Team
Management

BUSINESS MADE SIMPLE

Team
Management

Practical New Approaches

Charles Margerison
& Dick McCann

JAICO PUBLISHING HOUSE

Mumbai • Delhi • Bangalore • Kolkata
Hyderabad • Chennai • Ahmedabad • Bhopal

Published by Jaico Publishing House
121 Mahatma Gandhi Road
Mumbai - 400 023
jaicopub@vsnl.com
www.jaicobooks.com

Printed in arrangement with:
Management Books 2000 Ltd
Forge House, Limes Road
Kemble, Cirencester, Glos., GL7 6AD

Team Management
ISBN 81-7992-376-2

First Jaico Impression: 2005

Printed by
New Radharaman Printers
20, Wadala Udyog Bhavan
Wadala, Mumbai-400 031

CONTENTS

[v]

PREFACE

In 1982 we started collaborating on Team Management. Both of us were intrigued as to why some teams were highly successful and yet others failed even though the abilities of the individuals in both types of teams seemed to be about the same. Some groups of people seemed to be able to work together and develop synergy whereas others seemed to 'blow themselves apart'. It was to find the reasons for this that we embarked upon our research programme.

We have already published much concerning our Team Management work. However, many people have asked us to produce a book which has all of our team management ideas in the one volume – a volume that would be useful to both the human resources professional and the practising line manager.

There are many people who have helped us in our work and some of these are mentioned in the text. In particular, however, we would like to thank Rod Davies who has worked with us for nine years researching and validating the Team Management Index. He conducted a wide variety of psychometric assessments via the Institute of Team Management Studies and also supervised the work of other researchers who have contributed to the validation of the Team Management Index. In all of these activities he has shown what a good 'linker' can do to improve team performance. Chapter 9 is based on his research.

Others who have contributed to the validation studies under Rod's leadership are Rob Connelly, Gerry Corcoran, Angela McDonnell, and Geoff Carter. They have all been valuable Assessor-Developer and Controller-Inspector members of our team.

In addition we thank those who took the time to understand and back our work in the early days. In particular, Gordon Wills of MCB University Press showed entrepreneurial flair by providing an outlet through his organisation. Jacques Dufrenne, Bruno Dalbiez and Daniel Jeanrenaud of Hewlett-Packard have all been great supporters and we thank them for their confidence.

More recently Ian Gillies and Stewart Mitchell in Australia, Alan Barratt, Terry Mills and the UK Master Tutors have joined the TMS team on various occasions to conduct workshops. In addition the distributors of TMS throughout Europe have made the understanding of the TMS work more widely known.

We wish to thank Nick Wheeler for being the brains behind our software development, and also Alan Margerison for his important contribution.

In the USA we appreciate the support and entrepreneurial flair of Curtiss Peck of ASI. In Australia, Barrie Ffrench pioneered the use of the Team Management Index for recruitment and selection.

In New Zealand, Paul Robinson of Key Management Services has been an enthusiast for our work and has used Team Management Systems to help many New Zealand businesses. We also appreciate the managerial linking skills of Cathy Hick and her team which has contributed so much to the business development and client service arrangements, and now, in the USA, Jan Bearce and her team.

Much of our research work was carried out in Australia where Heather Burnett, Jan Stewart, Justin Walker-Jones,

Bronwyn Loudoun and Nikki Mead have all helped make TMS a well-known product.

There are many others who, along the way, have helped with a word of advice here, a constructive criticism there. Most of these people have been line managers. We thank you all, for without your interest and feedback we would not have been able to produce what is now acknowledged as a powerful and systematic approach to understanding Team Management.

Finally, thanks to our wives, Colinette and Dianne, and our own family teams who have supported us and had to manage without us on the numerous times we have had to travel in order to work with other teams.

Charles Margerison and Dick McCann
The Institute of Team Management Studies
April 1995

INTRODUCTION

This book provides a new approach to the development of high-performing teams. It examines the way in which you as an individual can understand your own strengths and use them in a team. It then shows how teams can work together effectively, particularly if they are well balanced and under the guidance of a 'managerial linker'. The book also outlines the way in which managers can develop effective work teams and the various organisational processes that need to be put in place for this to be achieved.

This book is the result of our work with more than 100,000 managers in the United Kingdom, the United States of America, Australia, South East Asia and Europe. Our work has been wide-ranging across many varied industry and service sectors. For example, we have worked with airline captains and their crews, helping them develop effective teamwork in the cockpit. It is absolutely vital from the time the crew come together to plan their flight, through to eventual touchdown and debriefing, that they have excellent teamwork.

We have also worked extensively in the manufacturing industries. Here we have enabled a number of project teams to devise new approaches to work improvement. This has involved working with teams from glass manufacturing plants, in brick-making factories, in the building industry, in engineering, as well as other aspects of production. We have also worked in chemical refineries where we have been asked to improve the way in which managers develop their teams to improve production, while maintaining an over-riding concern for safety.

Therefore the systems of 'Team Management' which we describe in this book have been employed in a wide range of industrial and commercial organisations. On each occasion the managers have told us that the systems have worked. That, we believe, is the highest praise that we can receive. At the end of the day it is the managers and their teams who must be the ultimate judges of the work that we are doing.

This book outlines the principles associated with concept of 'Team Management'. This was derived from our work with line managers. We listened to the key words they used to signal important aspects of work and built them into the Team Wheel. We have also been influenced by the work of Carl Jung on Psychological Types and also the work of Professor Reg Revans on Action Learning. The theoretical work of Jung and the practical work of Revans have been combined to produce systems that can be used in every facet of management.

Jung's 'psychological types' form the basis of the Team Management Index – an instrument designed to determine individual work preferences. This results in a personal 4000-word report highlighting individual strengths and weaknesses. Alongside the Team Management Index we have also created other 'vehicles' such as the Types of Work Index plus one on Linking and Teamwork. Probably the most important of these is the Team Management Wheel. This is a cognitive aid which managers can use to 'map' their own areas of preferred working and assess how well their team is balanced.

On the practical side we have been very active on designing ways in which a team can improve its own performance. Our work here is founded on the theories of group processes, combined with the work of Reg Revans on action learning. The action-learning philosophy is essentially based around the notion of managers meeting in teams, in a planned and systematic way, to help improve the way things are done. This may sound deceptively easy: however, we have found that it requires a great deal of thought, planning and organisation. We have identified the key principles in this book and show how they relate to our work on team role preferences.

Overall the result is a number of Team Management Systems which managers can use to develop their team into a high-performing unit. 'High performance' is not something simple that you can plug in and switch on. It requires a great deal of confidence and a willingness to involve all members of the team. It is not something that will happen overnight. There is no quick-fix instant solution. It requires a hard-nosed approach to resolving issues over a period of time.

This means that we have to start with the realities of life. We have to look at the problems as well as the opportunities. We have to take a set of objectives and convert them into projects which people can work upon. We have to provide them with a structure over and above that which they have for day-to-day operations. We have to provide them with opportunities to develop skills and abilities over and above what they possess now.

This, together with the individual development that comes from personal understanding, is what Team Management Systems are all about. They are a powerful approach to improvement. We hope that you enjoy learning about them in this book. and that they have a practical benefit in your own organisation.

Please find time to try out some of the ideas mentioned in this book. We are convinced you will be delighted with the results.

1

TEAM MANAGEMENT AT WORK

Why is team management important?

Success or failure in business is a result of whether people work together effectively in teams. Some organisations have a very good record in teamwork.

Therefore managers should regularly look at how they are managing their teams and constantly compare their performance against the best practice in the world. Only by doing this can organisations keep one step ahead of the competition.

Our work in organisations has been focused on improving team management and developing high-performance teams. We have worked in oil companies, airlines, banks, manufacturing organisations and many other wealth-producing organisations. It has led us to produce a new approach that has proven its value as an aid to managers in all of the industries mentioned. Specific examples from prominent organisations will be described as we proceed.

What do teams need in order to succeed?

We started our work in a practical way by talking to numerous managers about how they managed their teams – what problems they faced, how they tried to solve them, what results they achieved. As we discussed the issues we found the managers talking about the ways in which they wanted to improve their teams and develop better performing individuals.

As we listened, we began to identify critical areas of teamwork that recurred consistently. We heard such comments as:

- 'We are good on ideas but weak on implementation.'
- 'We are not as coordinated as we could be.'
- 'We are strong on the control side of the job but don't adapt well to change.'
- 'We need to understand each other more.'
- 'We require better back-up support to our field people.'
- 'I would like to improve our communication.'
- 'We need to involve people more in decisions.'

Gradually a picture began to emerge of what managers felt were the essential functions for teamwork. They emphasised the need for all-round skills and teams that could be flexible in order to meet changing situations. The comparison seemed very similar to sporting teams where you need attackers and defenders, but often those that are strong in 'shooting' are not strong in 'tackling' and vice versa. In short, there are key teamwork functions which can be identified and developed.

We also looked at examples of critical situations where teamwork meant literally the difference between life and death. Because one of our major clients was a large airline (Australian Airlines) we read the transcripts of what the 'black box' recorders showed to be the last few minutes of flights that did not make it. Many show lack of teamwork to be a significant contributory factor in many accidents and crashes. Overall it has been estimated that over 70 per cent of all airline accidents and crashes are a function of communication rather than technical factors. Below is one example where more effective teamwork communication could have saved lives.

Cockpit decisions – teamwork on the flight deck

It was seven degrees below zero on a January day in 1982. Air Florida Flight 90 was preparing to take off from Washington National Airport. For over 20 minutes in the taxi approach to the runway the two pilots had shared views on the conditions. The co-pilot expressed doubts but the captain did not seem to respond.

The throttles are pushed forward; Air Florida Flight 90 accelerates down runway 36.

'God, look at that thing! That don't seem right, does it. Ah, that's not right,' said Roger Pettit, First Officer flying the leg.

'Yes, it is, there's eighty (knots),' replied Larry Wheaton, the plane's 34-year-old captain.

'Naw, I don't think that's right. Ah, maybe it is ....'

Twenty-two seconds later the 737-222 struggles into the air, barely able to climb. In just 30 more seconds the aircraft will crash into the barrier wall of the northbound span of the Fourteenth Street Bridge which connects Virginia to the District of Columbia. By the time the aircraft has settled in the frozen Potomac River on the west side of the bridge, 78 people will have died, including Pettit, Wheaton and four motorists innocently crossing into Arlington County.

The National Transportation Safety Board, an independent federal agency that examines all civil aviation accidents, decided that flight crew teamwork was the probable cause of the crash, including the decision to take off with snow and ice on the plane and Wheaton's failure to stop the take-off despite four warnings from Pettit that instrument readings indicated engine problems.

[3]

Bay of Pigs – lack of political teamwork

It is also worth looking at some other cases of teamwork failure. One of the most celebrated teamwork errors in the political arena was the so-called Bay of Pigs fiasco. On 17 April 1961 John F. Kennedy, US President, had given the approval for a brigade of 1400 Cuban exiles to be landed on a swampy coast of the Bay of Pigs in Cuba. The US navy, air force and the CIA were committed to the overthrow of the Cuban leader Fidel Castro.

Nothing went right. On the first day not one of the four supply ships carrying essential supplies and munitions arrived in Cuba. The first two were destroyed by Castro's supposedly weak air force and the other two promptly fled. By nightfall on the second day, the brigade was completely surrounded by 20,000 soldiers in Castro's well-equipped army. On the third day the 1200 remaining insurgents were captured and ignominiously led off to prison camps. Seven months later, Castro extracted a hard bargain from the US State Department, receiving $53 million ransom in food and drugs.

After the event analysis, commentators and even Kennedy himself could not understand how a decision was made to proceed with the invasion. Any serious analysis of the assumptions underlying the Bay of Pigs operation should have highlighted the incredible risk involved and the questionable nature of the propositions on which the invasion was founded.

The group that deliberated the Bay of Pigs decision was Kennedy's inner-circle advisory team. They had considerable intellectual talent and, like the President, were shrewd politicians capable of objective, rational analysis. Yet collectively they failed to detect serious flaws in the invasion and gave their approval to an operation so ill-conceived that even today the name 'Bay of Pigs' is a symbol for the perfect failure.

[4]

Boardroom decisions – teamwork at senior levels

Teamwork failure often occurs in the boardrooms of companies. Consider the following real-life case from industry and see how you respond.

Imagine you are in the boardroom of a large computer retailer. The finance director is proposing a severe cost containment programme to counteract a fall in market sales of the company's range of personal computers. The chairman, research director and senior store managers agree but Tony Collins, the marketing manager, proposes an expansion in operations and a move into IBM PCs, which he sees as sweeping the business world.

Collins's temerity in suggesting this 'outlandish' proposal is rewarded with immediate opposition and a hasty rejection on the grounds that 'we must hang on to what we've got'. The Chairman reiterates that the cost structure of the whole enterprise must be examined with a 'fine-tooth comb' before any change in company policy is considered. Recognising defeat, Collins falls in with the group's decision.

Twelve months later the company closes its doors – a victim of the high-tech revolution where product life cycles of less than a year are not uncommon.

The common thread

What do the above examples have in common? In every case faulty decisions have been made because of poor teamwork.

Today's world is so complex and fast-moving that it is virtually impossible for important decisions to be made by one person. Team decisions are practised every day in government, on the flight deck and in boardrooms and yet in most cases the 'players' have little understanding of team dynamics and how to use a team to advantage. As a result poor decisions are often made.

The failure of Kennedy's inner circle to defeat any of the false assumptions behind the Bay of Pigs invasion can at least partially be accounted for by the group's tendency to seek consensus at the expense of sharing information and conducting a critical debate and analysis. The consensus-seeking tendency manifested itself in 'shared illusions' and other symptoms which contributed to over-confidence in the face of vague uncertainties and explicit warn-ings that should have alerted the members to the risks of clandes-tine military operations.

Group-think

Janis (1972), in his book *Victims of Group-Think*, hypothesises a number of reasons as to why the Bay of Pigs decision was made. In particular he cites the 'illusion of invulnerability' and the 'illu-sion of unanimity 'as important factors in the decision process. As one Justice Department spokesman said:

> It seemed that with John Kennedy leading us and with all the talent he had assembled, nothing could stop us. We believed that if we faced up to the nation's problems and applied bold new ideas with common sense and hard work, we would over-come whatever challenged us.

Janis continues:

> When a group of people who respect each other's opinions arrives at a unanimous view each member is likely to feel that the belief must be true. This reliance on consensus validation tends to replace individual critical thinking and reality testing, unless there are clearcut disagreements among the members. The members of a face-to-face group often become inclined, without realising it, to prevent latent disagreements from surfacing, when they are about to initiate a risky course of action.

Officially, other reasons were given for the Bay of Pigs fiasco and all of them were undoubtedly contributory. In particular the problems of a new administration working with an old bureaucracy were highlighted by official sources. It was claimed that Kennedy did not get to know the strengths and weaknesses of his newly appointed advisers, and if he had only had time to assess his team then the mistake might not have been made.

On Air Florida Flight 90 the illusion of invulnerability may also have been operating. Many pilots and industry observers who heard Pettit and Wheaton's conversation played back from the plane's 'black box' recorder commented on the casual nature of the conversation. As one pilot has said to us:

> It seems as though they did not understand how serious the problem was but it is my bet that they did. When you have been flying successfully for many years you start to believe it can't happen to me.
>
> Unless pilots are trained in teamwork there may be a tendency to keep fears and worries to oneself. If we don't speak up and share our information then how can we make the right decision? So many things are going on when an incident occurs that all crew members need to be actively involved in solving the problem.

Certainly there was a serious lack of teamwork on Flight AF90. Not only did the First Officer say four times that things weren't right prior to the critical take-off speed but five times during the taxi-period he expressed his worries about ice on the wings ... and yet they went ahead with the flight. They may have shared information reasonably well but they failed to analyse the situation adequately.

In the boardroom of the computer company we are faced with a team of people who are fairly similar in their outlook – 'down-to-earth', practical, analytical, detail-oriented executives who think alike. When faced with someone who presents a proposal opposed to their normal way of thinking their immediate reaction is to label the idea 'ridiculous'. When several members endorse this view, the group tends to believe they must be right and a

[7]

potentially valuable proposal is ignored and not even discussed
or analysed as a serious alternative.

The need for teamwork

'Teamwork' is the key to modern management. From the
'Eyewitness Team' bringing you the latest television news to
projects designed and developed by construction groups,
management world-wide is realising the power of a 'well-oiled'
team. No longer can decisions be made solely by one person.

In high-tech businesses, for example, a wide range of multi-
disciplinary skills is often required, ranging from biotechnology
through to electronic engineering and accounting. Managers can't
be skilled in all these areas and therefore they must rely on teamwork.

Social scientists who have studied more objectively the way
managers work have mirrored this new concern by turning their
attention from the individual focus on leadership to a group focus
on team behaviour and group dynamics.

Successful managers will work through the team and their
success will depend upon the team succeeding. A team is more
than a number of brilliant individual advisers. It is a group of
people who understand each other, who know individual
strengths and weaknesses and who cooperate with one another.

As Lee Iacocca, the CEO of the Chrysler Corporation, says in
his autobiography (Iacocca, 1986):

> In the end, all business operations can be reduced to three
> words: people, product and profit. People come first. Unless
> you've got a good team you can't do much with the other two.

The main job of team leaders is to get the group performing at a
high level. They need to spend the greater part of their time
managing the group and above all they must have a firm understanding of the theory of Team Management.

A team of brilliant individuals can often be less effective than a brilliant team of individuals. This is part of the reason why 'think-tanks' are often unsuccessful. It is not enough to simply assemble the best minds in the organisation or the country. Sound principles of Team Management need to be applied as well.

Developing team management systems

Enabling people to work together well is the key job of every manager. To do this requires more than technical ability or high intelligence. It requires systems of team management that can be operated on a regular basis.

These must be defined, communicated and worked upon by all members. Above all, team members must develop team management skills and practise them in a disciplined fashion until they work easily and well together. Nothing can be left to chance. Good habits must be developed and maintained. This book is about how to win through the implementation of these effective team management systems.

2

TEAM MANAGEMENT SKILLS

How effective teams work

Each year thousands of people visit Disneyland and Disneyworld. They see the cartoon characters such as Mickey Mouse and Donald Duck come to life. Behind the fantasy, however, lies the hard work – developing and managing a team of people.

We have studied a number of successful people and looked at how they have built up their organisations. A classic example is Walt Disney and his brother Roy.

Walt Disney started as a creative artist with lots of ideas, but little money. He indicated how he got started:

When I was in high school in Chicago, I went to art school three nights a week. My first job as an artist getting paid for the stuff was when I was 18, at an advertising agency. I was their flunkey at $50 a month. In February 1920 a film company wanted an Artist First Class. The 'first class' didn't bother me at all. On my own I had set up selling to the guys doing the oil journals. My work was printed. That's how I got into this business. (McDonald, 1975.)

However, behind Walt Disney, the creative artist, was Roy Disney. He had a very different range of skills and approach to getting things done. He never became as famous as his brother, but Roy Disney was a key factor in their success. McDonald notes: 'They were a lifetime team, with Roy taking care of the financial end of the business.'

The whole idea of teamwork can be seen in the way the Disney brothers worked together and developed their organisation. While they were different, they complemented each other's skills. This is a characteristic that we have always found in successful teams.

All of us have been members of a team at some time in our lives. Growing up in a family team, for example, or playing in a sports team are ways in which we have worked with others. A key characteristic of a team is that the members have a common purpose and depend upon each other for the ultimate performance. At work, most jobs are done on an individual basis, but the total effort defines the 'teamwork'.

Usually, no one person by himself can do all the jobs required. It was Lord Wilfred Brown, the ex-managing director of the Glacier Metal Company, who stressed that managers only had their jobs because there was too much work for them to do by themselves and they had to appoint people to share the tasks under their direction and guidance.

The very success of our modern way of living depends upon teamwork. Organisations that produce the goods and services that we take for granted are structured in teams, each having their own objectives and areas of accountability. Managers all have different approaches to making their teams successful. However, they agree that the end purpose must be to achieve a winning combination where individuals work together to meet the task objectives. The role of the manager in this process is critical. Often

[11]

there are lots of highly talented individuals, but they need a skilled manager to bring them together as a team.

Sporting teams

It is easy to see the concept of high-performing teams in the context of sport. Competing against other teams on a regular basis, where there are points available for wins, losses and draws, provides a measure of success and attainment. Indeed the whole concept of sporting teams provides a good basis for improving managerial effectiveness. The comparisons are clear. Any team can 'win' only if it uses the abilities of the members in a coordinated effort rather than in a series of individual activities. Whereas one or two individuals may shine above the others, at the end of the day a team wins consistently because the team members complement each other.

Furthermore, the sporting context illustrates the competitive nature of activity. In this sense, it is a microcosm of the work environment. A team, whether it be playing football, baseball, basketball, or any such game, ultimately has one objective – to score more than the opposition. So it is in the work situation, even though the lines may not be quite as dearly defined. One organisation in the furniture industry is competing with another organisation in the same industry. Car companies in one country, such as the United States, are competing with car companies in Japan, for example. Increasingly, competition in most industries is becoming fierce. Therefore, while any individual team may not see its opponents, they are nevertheless 'in competition'. Japanese car workers may not see or meet the American car worker, but their efforts as part of a team are seen in terms of the output and results. The effort therefore that goes into teamwork these days is crucial to business success.

However, sports teams can only succeed if they are balanced. It is no use having a team which is strong in defence but has no attack. Equally, a team will fail if they are good on the left side of the field, but poor on the right side. So it is with industrial teams – they too must be well balanced. They must have people who are able to look after detail at one end, while at the opposite end others should be able to explore and develop new initiatives.

Work teams – the key work functions

If organisational work teams need a balance to be 'the best' – then what should this balance consist of? To answer this question we embarked on a research study to characterise the key work activities that need to go on in a team if it is to be effective. We talked with many 'high-performing' teams and listened to what they had to say about the way they approached their work.

In the end we were able to identify nine key activities or 'work functions' that need to be present if the team is to optimise its performance. These work functions are generic and are independent of the technical functions that may have to go on in the team. Therefore they apply to all teams, be they in accounting, engineering, research and development, marketing or some other area. These nine work functions form the basis of our theory of Team Management. They emerge from discussing the critical success factors with people in factories, offices, laboratories, banks, airlines and other work locations.

Advising

Advising is all about gathering and giving information. Some people such as librarians, researchers, or information officers love gathering all sorts of data and presenting it back to others. Often it is the starting point for launching a new product or service, where information is sought about competitors or new products being launched in other parts of the world.

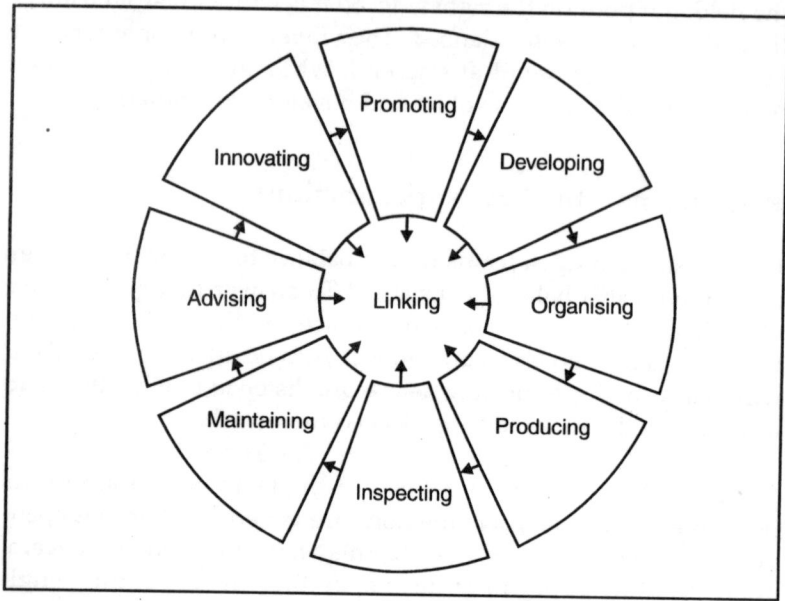

Figure 1. Types of work.

Innovating

Innovating is all about creating new ideas or thinking up new ways of tackling old problems. Some people, like research and development scientists, may spend 80 per cent or so of their time in this area whereas other people, concerned say with production, may have little chance to work in the innovating area. Nonetheless, it is a very important element of most jobs. The failure to innovate will sooner or later lead to organisational failure.

Promoting

People who are involved in promoting-type work usually enjoy looking for new opportunities and persuading others. Maybe information about a new market potential has been gathered and

[14]

some researcher has dreamed up a novel way of exploiting the opportunity. However, it is up to the promoter to sell the idea to management and to gather all the resources – money, equipment, people – to get the job under way. All jobs have an element of promoting in them. Some people are good at it and others shy away from the up-front people-contact that is required.

Developing

Once an idea has been generated and 'sold' to management, development takes place. Here the initial concept is exposed to a vigorous analytical process and developed to a stage where it has a chance of succeeding in the market place. Creativity is often required here as in 'innovating' work but the main difference is in the applied nature of the work as the 'developer' needs to have one eye on the realities of the market place and plan out the way to apply the ideas.

Organising

Many jobs have an element of organising associated with them. Organising is all about setting up a structure and resources so that the product, scheme, or service can work. It involves managing the resources to get the tasks done. Deadlines need to be established and performance benchmarks set so that the goals of the team, division or organisation can be achieved. Some people enjoy the 'cut and thrust' that is often associated with organising whereas others find it difficult to deal with the hard decisions that are often required.

Producing

Producing is usually the heart and soul of most organisations. After all, it is the regular production of the goods or services that brings in the bottom-line profit. People working in production may spend most of their time working in this area but all teams, even research and development teams, will have some element of production associated with the work they do.

Inspecting

When goods or services are being produced on a regular basis there is always a need to ensure that the 'details' are watched. High quality has to be maintained and accurate records of the financial position kept. This is the inspecting type of work characteristically done by people such as accountants, quality controllers and clerks. Contracts have to be set and monitored. Procedures have to be fulfilled to comply with safety, security and other regulatory areas.

Maintaining

'Maintaining' is a work category we have found common to all jobs. It is to do with ensuring that the infrastructure is in place so that the team, division or organisation can work with maximum efficiency. In general it is associated with the support services offered in an organisation and the general background work done in a team to ensure that its requirements can be met quickly and efficiently. The result is an emphasis on standards, on quality and a code of principles to govern behaviour at work.

Linking

The last work function category is shown in the middle of the Types of Work Wheel because it is central to the success of all teams. Someone has to coordinate all the team members to ensure that there is maximum cooperation and interchange of ideas, reports and experiences.

The linking function often means the difference between effective and ineffective teams. Often a team may have members who are highly skilled and individually capable but unless someone is performing the linking function the team is likely to fail.

Most managers have found the Types of Work Wheel an extremely useful representation of the work activities of a high-performing team, whether these teams are whole organisations, divisions, sections, task forces or smaller work groups. We shall show how you can use this team management approach to develop systems to ensure your team works together effectively.

Team assessment example

An example of how this can be done using the Team Management Wheel is the approach used in a large manufacturing company. For some time the senior manager had been concerned that his team members were not working together effectively. There had been numerous examples of deadlines being missed, poor quality work, interpersonal arguments and a lack of new ideas.

The general manager therefore brought the team together and as an introduction had one of our team discuss the Types of Work Wheel. This led on immediately to a discussion on 'What areas do we need to be strong in to meet the challenges in our business?'

The team agreed the need was to be strong in creating, promoting and developing, given the rapid changes in markets and products.

They completed a questionnaire of ours and gained feedback on their own preferences and strengths. They quickly came to the conclusion they were good at organising, producing and inspecting. This led to a deep discussion on how to improve in the areas that were perceived as weak. They concluded they should put more time and effort into those areas and go out and seek training as appropriate.

They also concluded that the conflicts between those who

wanted to spend more time on innovating and those who wanted to maintain the status quo so that the production system was not disturbed, should cease.

The team set objectives to improve their performance in the key areas and then met again a few months later to assess progress. Again they used the same system, having the work functions as a point for reference and comparison. The general feeling was that they were more effective and placing their efforts in a more relevant way.

Understanding team roles

It is clear from the manufacturing case that a team can improve its performance if it has a way of identifying where its weaknesses are, and has the chance to discuss and implement improvements.

The Types of Work Wheel and its derivative the Team Management Wheel (see Chapter 3) are a basis for diagnosing how well a team is performing. The key activities needed in the team can be analysed and then roles and responsibilities assigned so that these activities are covered by the team members best equipped to deal with them.

In this regard we developed the concept of *work preferences* and an understanding of these is fundamental to the success of a team.

3

MEASURING WORK PREFERENCES

Introduction

When we discussed with managers the key activities that need to go on in a team we found that they indicated preferences for some activities and dislikes for others. One manager said:

> I really enjoy the innovating and promoting aspects of my job but I'm not very interested in the detail (inspecting work). Often I gloss over the details or try to delegate them to others. It is the generation of ideas that motivates and enthuses me.

Another said:

> What is important to me is that the job is delivered on time and to high standards of accuracy. This is where I concentrate a lot of my energies. Sometimes I have difficulty working with these 'ideas people' who are always thinking up new ways of improving things and as a result there are no outputs delivered.

[19]

It became clear to us that people do have work preferences – that is, work they choose to do or not to do. The Types of Work Wheel is therefore a useful way of presenting these activities. Most people we talked to said that there was at least three areas, sometimes four, where they felt really 'at home'. Usually there were one or more areas that they disliked or preferred not to be involved in. As a result they often delegated these activities to others or gave them a low priority.

Given that all the work functions are necessary for a team to be high-performing we then thought: 'Wouldn't it be a good idea if we could identify a person's work function preference?' If, for example, someone prefers promoting work, then we could look at ways of ensuring that this person covered many of the promoting activities of the team. In this way their skills would be used to advantage. Usually people practise what they prefer and therefore perform better in those areas that match their preference.

To identify work preferences we developed an instrument called the Margerison-McCann Team Management Index. This is a 60-item questionnaire that enables managers and their teams to gather important information on the personal strengths and weaknesses of each person. The Team Management Index (TMI) provides a means of understanding which of the work functions are of high and low interest. In this chapter we shall outline how this is done and show its value in systematic team development.

What determines work preferences

Given that different managers demonstrate varying preferences for the 'type of work' they engage in, we began to ask ourselves how these differences came about.

In trying to explain them, we were guided in our work by the writings of C. J. Jung (1923) who, more than 60 years ago, suggested that several key factors might explain many of the differences between people. While examining his ideas, we found a clear relevance to the work of managers, and began to adapt his earlier concepts in explaining individual work preferences in a similar way to that adopted by Myers-Briggs (1962, 1977), whose work was initially developed as a career guidance mechanism for adolescents.

The key difference in our work is that we have focused exclusively on the work situation.

Four key work questions

In our work with managers four key issues began to emerge.

1. How do people prefer to relate with others?
2. How do people prefer to gather and use information?
3. How do people prefer to make decisions?
4. How do people prefer to organise themselves and others?

Each day at work we have to deal with these four questions. The first question is all about *relationships*. Some people are outgoing and sociable in their relationships and relate with others in an extroverted way whereas others are quieter and do not have a high need to be with people, i.e. they tend to relate in an introverted way. This clearly affects their work in a team and we built this into our method of assessment.

The second question relates to *information management*. When people gather and use information they often have a preference to be either practical or creative. Practical people prefer to work with tested ideas and pay attention to the facts and detail, whereas creative people are often challenging the status quo and coming up with new ideas.

The third area relates to *decision-making*. When decisions are made they are normally made either in an analytical way or according to an individual's beliefs. Analytical people will set up objective decision criteria and choose that decision which maximises the pay-off, whereas beliefs-oriented people will tend to make decisions which accord with their own personal principles and values.

Finally, the fourth question relates to *organisational* issues. Managers seem to organise themselves and others in a structured or flexible way. Structured people are action-oriented and like to conclude or resolve issues, whereas flexible people like to spend time diagnosing the situation and will tend to put off 'concluding' and 'resolving' until they have gathered all the information they can.

Time and time again we found the validity of these four critical managerial areas and their associated preferences confirmed by groups of managers. We therefore decided to use them as a way of measuring which parts of the Types of Work Wheel managers preferred. These preferences are shown in Figure 2 and form the basis for the Team Management Index constructs.

We have found that managers identify with our classification very readily. As we gathered data on people's preferences according to the scales, several observations began to emerge. One of the most important was that the four scales were fairly independent. In other words, the fact that someone might be more extroverted does not mean that they are more likely to be practical rather than creative. Similarly, there was no relationship between practical people and whether they had a preference for analytical or beliefs-oriented decision-making.

Once we were convinced that these four key areas of management preference accurately described various management styles, we then considered how they might relate to the Types of Work Wheel. Would, for example, an extroverted, creative, analytical and flexible approach to work describe someone with a preference for promoting or organising or even inspecting? Would an introverted, practical, beliefs-orientated and highly structured person prefer inspecting work or promoting work or even advising work? Would these two very different kinds of people work together well?

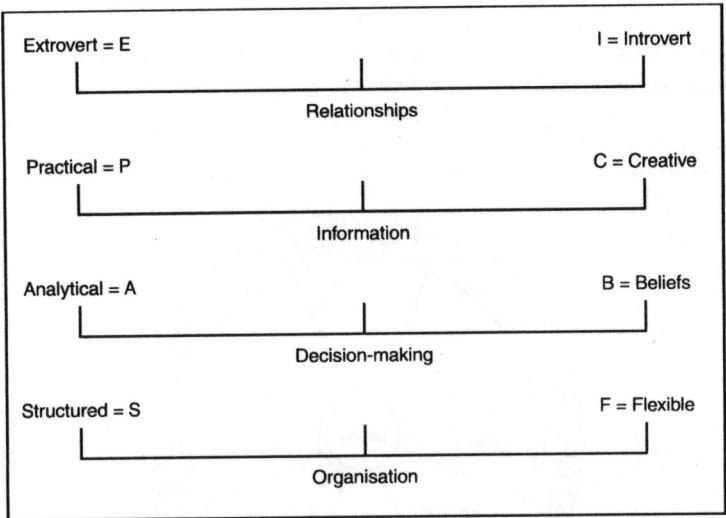

Figure 2. Key managerial work areas and their associated work preferences.

After a very detailed analysis we were able to show that there was indeed a valid relationship between the Types of Work Wheel and a person's work preferences. This relationship enabled us to develop the Team Management Wheel.

The Team Management Wheel

The Team Management Wheel provides an integrated map of people's work preferences and relates them to the key roles that are necessary in a high-performing team. A person's set of four preferences can be mapped on to the Wheel, highlighting those functions in which they prefer to work.

Thus the two aspects of our research – 'types of work' and work preferences – are combined into the Team Management Wheel, a practical model which can be used in a variety of management development applications. Each sector of the Wheel has certain preferences associated with it. For example, our statistical research,

[23]

reported later, suggested that people with a preference for the 'promoting' work function were, amongst other things, more likely to have high extroverted and creative scores whereas those who enjoyed 'producing' were more likely to have high practical and structured scores.

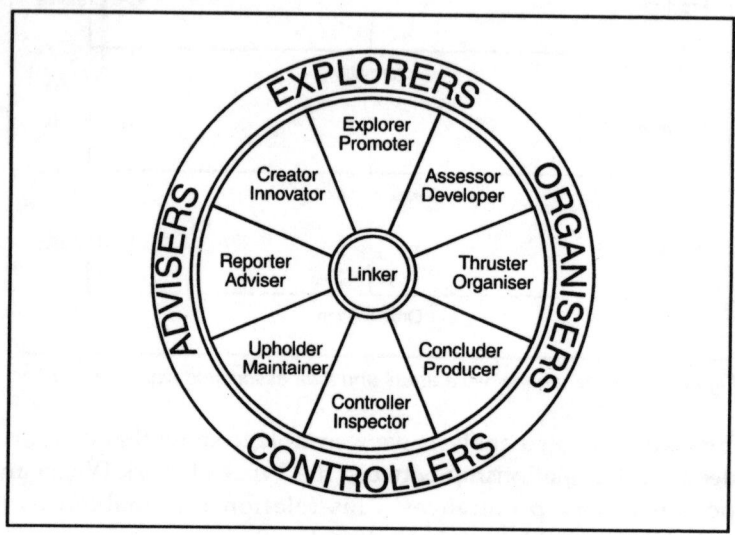

Figure 3. The Margerison-McCann Team Management Wheel.

The Wheel has eight sectors and a hub just like the Types of Work Wheel, but because it now describes work functions and preferences we find it more convenient to present it as a model of 'team roles' where each sector describes not only the work function enjoyed but also the behavioural characteristics associated with someone preferring that sector. For that reason each sector contains a behavioural description, e.g. 'Thruster', as well as the defining work function of 'Organiser'. Each role area therefore has a two-word description such as Creator-Innovator, Concluder-Producer and so on. For example:

- Advisers enjoy reporting data.
- Innovators enjoy creating ideas.

- Promoters enjoy exploring opportunities.
- Developers enjoy assessing plans.
- Organisers enjoy thrusting into action.
- Producers enjoy concluding tasks.
- Inspectors enjoy controlling procedures.
- Maintainers enjoy upholding standards.

Around the rim of the Wheel are found major activities such as:

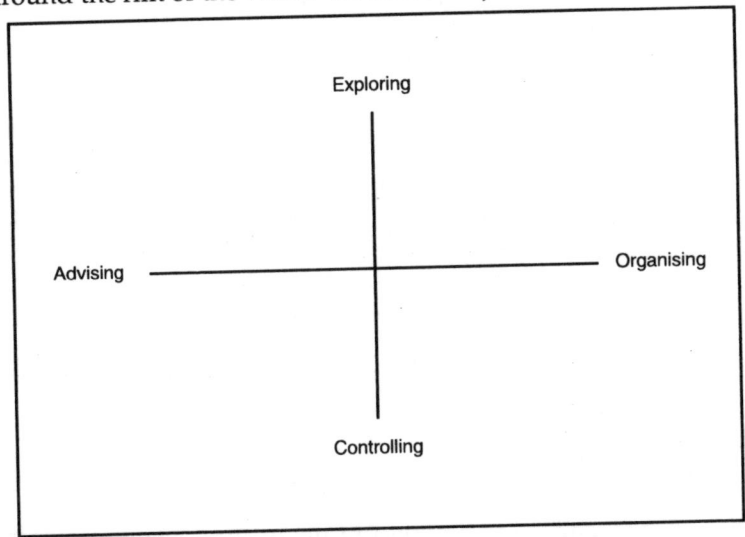

In short, people can prefer either a job which has a strong element of control or one where there is a high degree of exploring and looking for new opportunities. Some people prefer both exploring and controlling, but usually we have found people to have more preference one way or the other: maybe 60-40 in one direction or 70-30 in the other.

Moving towards the centre of the wheel we can see that these four major activities are expanded into eight roles. These are known as 'role preferences' or 'team roles' and are made up of different combinations of the various work preferences discussed earlier.

In the centre of the wheel is the Linker role. This role is one which can be learned from experience in coordinating and integrating groups of people. We shall have more to say on the role of the Linker later. However, at this point it is important to stress that the Linker is not a work preference but a set of skills which all people can develop. Thus the Linker role may be held in conjunction with any one of the eight major role preferences.

Let us now look at how you can measure work preferences using what for short we call the TMI.

The Team Management Index (TMI)

The TMI is a 60-item normative, forced-choice instrument which measures work preferences along the four key factors of relationships, information, decisions and organisation. The scores on these constructs are then mapped on to the Team Management Wheel, resulting in a major role preference and two related roles. For each of the 60 questions, participants are asked to choose between two preferred ways of working. For example, Item 15 of the TMI reads:

A	B
I prefer possibilities.....	I prefer .....realities

You can then choose to respond in one of four ways, assigning values of 2, 1 or 0 to either side:

A	B	Meaning
2	0	I definitely prefer possibilities
2	1	I prefer possibilities but realities are important to me
1	2	I prefer realities but possibilities are important to me
0	2	I definitely prefer realities

The 60 items have been drawn from statements made by managers about their work either informally, in meetings, or in management training and development programmes, and assessed for their reliability and validity. As a result, the terms and language are familiar to managers and easy to understand. Fifteen questions assess a person's score on each of the four constructs.

The scores on each scale range over 30 points either side of the centre point. In some situations a manager may respond on the right-hand side of the range and in other situations the left-hand side may be preferred. For example, in some situations managers will prefer to be more extroverted, while in others they will prefer to be more introverted. The TMI allows such differences in choice to be reflected. Therefore a person may score 18 on the Extroversion scale and 12 on the Introversion side. This shows the range of preference. For purposes of analysis this person would receive an overall assessment as being more of an Extrovert as this is the choice that predominates in the way he or she responds to the Index.

Generally a respondent's score consists of the first letter of the appropriate pole signifying the direction of the preference and a number signifying the magnitude of a preference. This is repeated for each scale, resulting in four 'preference scores'.

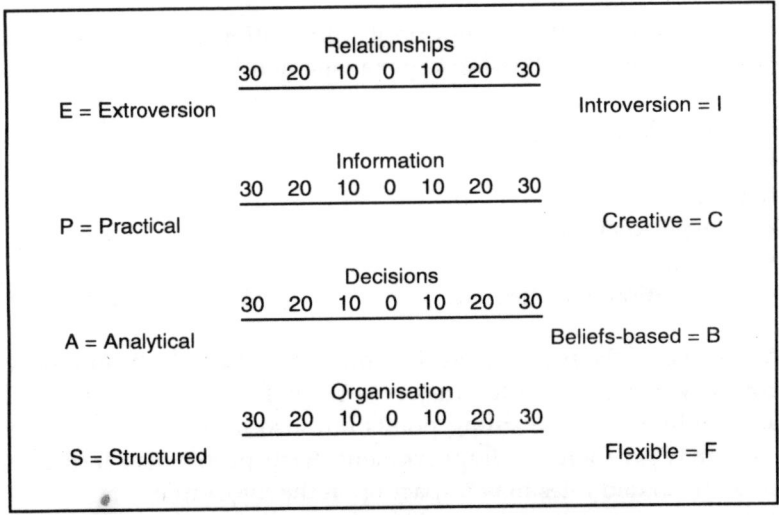

Figure 4. The Team Management Index scoring scale.

[27]

For example, a person who scores E-20, C-5, B-10 and F-7 would have agreed with many more of the Extrovert responses than the Introvert, more of the Creative than the Practical responses, more of the Beliefs than the Analytical and more of the Flexible than the Structured responses. They would then map on to the Team Management Wheel into the Creator-Innovator sector with related roles of Reporter-Adviser and Explorer-Promoter. (Refer to Chapter 9 on Research Data for an explanation of this mapping.)

Team Management Profiles

The scores on the four work preference constructs will determine the Team Management Profile that is received. Currently there are 208 different combinations possible in the Team Management Systems software and each person receives one of these 4000-word reports. If you wish to receive your own Team Management Profile then please contact one of the addresses at the back of this book.

The profile contains important information about individual preferences in the following key management areas:

- self-understanding
- decision-making
- team-building
- interpersonal skills
- organisation
- information management

At the end of the profile there are between 20 and 30 key summary points which describe the major work preferences. The personal profiles highlight the strong points but also indicate areas where there may be room for improvement. Each profile also indicates how the related roles may impact upon the major role.

Brief summaries of the profiles are given below to show some of the major characteristics of each section of the wheel. These summaries illustrate some of the major preferences but are not intended as feedback data. This can only be done accurately through a personal profile received when a TMI is completed.

Brief descriptions of role preferences

Creator-Innovators

Creator-Innovators are people who have a number of ideas which may well challenge and upset the existing way of doing things. Such people can be very independent and wish to experiment and pursue their ideas regardless of present systems and methods. They therefore need to be managed in such a way that their ideas have every opportunity to develop unfettered by organisational constraints; otherwise they are likely to feel inhibited and their creative output may decrease. Many organisations set up research and development units (often separated from the production units) to allow people to experiment with their ideas.

However, on every team it is important to have people who are more ideas-orientated and to give them and others the opportunity to talk through their views, even though it may seem at the time to be disturbing the existing way of operating. Such people will provide new ways of thinking and often 'way-out' ideas which may make it difficult for them to fit easily into a stable systematic operation. As team members they should be encouraged rather than 'put down' for their unusual, often challenging, thoughts, but in such a way that they can evolve their ideas in the light of practical reality.

Explorer-Promoters

Explorer-Promoters are usually excellent at both generating ideas and getting people enthusiastic about them. They will go out and find what is happening outside the organisation and compare new ideas with what is being done by other people. They are also good at bringing back contacts, information and resources which can help innovation in the team. They are very capable of pushing an idea forward even if they are not always the best people to organise and control it.

They are usually influential, talk easily, even on subjects where they are not expert, and enjoy searching for new opportunities and challenges. They can become easily bored and therefore like the challenge of moving from one project to another. They are particularly good at absorbing ideas from others (Creator-Innovators, for example) and promoting them enthusiastically to others.

Assessor-Developers

Assessor-Developers provide a balance between the 'exploring' and 'organising' parts of the Team Management Wheel. Often they look for ways and means of making an idea work in practice. Their concern is to see if the market wants the innovation and they will therefore test it against some practical criteria. Very often they will produce a prototype or do a market research study. Their whole interest is in developing an innovation to the point where there is a plan showing it can work. In this regard they are excellent 'reality-testers' and are unlikely to get carried away with ideas as sometimes happens with Explorer-Promoters and Creator-Innovators.

However, once they have given ideas the 'practical twist' to make them work in practice, they may well lose interest in the project and prefer to move off and work on another idea or project. The 'producing' function they prefer to leave to others.

Thruster-Organisers

Thruster-Organisers are the people who will get things done. Once they have been convinced that the 'idea' is of interest they will set up procedures and systems and turn the idea into a working reality. They will arrange and organise people and systems to ensure that deadlines can be met.

They put emphasis on getting things done even if it does mean that on the way certain 'feathers are ruffled'. They set objectives, establish plans, work out who should do what and then press hard to get results.

They may at times be impatient when people or things get in their way, but being Thruster-Organisers they will go through obstacles if they can't get round them. They are task-orientated, like to work to timed deadlines and seek to control their world rather than let it control them.

Concluder-Producers

Concluder-Producers take a great pride in producing a product or service to a standard. They will do this on a regular basis and feel fulfilled if they can deliver 'what is expected, when it is expected'. Indeed, they like working to set procedures and doing things in a regular way. The fact that they produced something yesterday does not mean they will be bored with producing it tomorrow. High standards of effectiveness and efficiency are important to them and their motto may well be 'if a job is worth doing it is worth doing well'.

Concluder-Producers have different preferences to Creator-Innovators, who dislike doing similar things day after day and want the variety and challenge of doing things differently. For Concluder-Producers the important thing is to use one's existing skills rather than continually changing and learning new ways of doing things. They therefore enjoy reproducing things and achieving the plans and goals they set.

Controller-Inspectors

Controller-Inspectors are people who enjoy doing detailed work and making sure that the facts and figures are correct. They will be careful and meticulous and often critical of errors or unsystematic work. Indeed, one of their great strengths is that they can concentrate for long periods of time upon a particular task, often working alone in their quiet individualistic way to ensure procedures are fulfilled.

This contrasts with the Explorer-Promoters, who continually need a wide variety of tasks and involvement with people. Controller-Inspectors are more likely to pursue matters in depth and make sure that the work is done according to plan in an accurate way. They pick up matters of detail quickly and can spot variances and errors with ease. For example, they are extremely valuable in financial and quality issues where an exacting eye for detail is required in order to detect errors and improve performance. All teams need people who will ensure this important work is done.

Upholder-Maintainers

Upholder-Maintainers are usually people of strong conviction about the way things should be done. They are often the people most supportive of others in the team and can provide a lot of stability.

They will defend the team against criticism and can be bitter opponents if you happen to be on the 'other side of the fence'. If you agree with their beliefs and feelings they are extremely helpful and will work tirelessly and unselfishly to assist you.

Their work preference is to consolidate – to make sure everything is in order and working well before pressing on. They can therefore be reluctant to make changes unless it is absolutely necessary. They prefer to work in a control-orientated, supportive way, making sure that things are done in accordance with their standards.

Alongside this they may prefer the advisory support role rather than the executive leading role. Therefore many people who have this preference will play more of a 'back room', helping

[32]

role, making sure that their case is well researched and documented. If asked, they will represent their team in negotiations and be difficult people to 'move' if they believe in the issues put forward.

Upholder-Maintainers are loyal to organisations whose values match their own deeply-seated beliefs. Usually they have a strong sense of what is 'right' or 'wrong' and are often driven by their own code of ethics, concern for quality and high standards.

Reporter-Advisers

Those who have a Reporter-Adviser work preference are good at generating information and gathering it together in such a way that it can be understood. Such people are usually patient, and prepared to hold off making a decision until they know as much as they can about the work to be done.

Some people may feel that Reporter-Advisers put things off until they really know matters in detail. However, to the Reporter-Adviser it is better to put forward a lot of information rather than present advice which is later seen to be inadequate. Such people are invaluable as 'support' members of the team, but they are not likely to be the people who will be strongly interested in organising others. Indeed, their concern is to make sure that all the information is available so that the 'best' decision can be made. They will particularly enjoy assignments which involve finding out as much as possible about a given situation. Often the role of a consultant or counsellor will come to them naturally.

Reporter-Advisers often make excellent facilitators and are amongst the most liked people in an organisation because of their interest in people and their willingness to listen with a 'sympathetic ear'.

[33]

Are all the profiles different?

For each of the eight major role preferences there are many major variations and combinations as to how people prefer to work in a team.

Basically for each sector there are two major variations in the team role and thirteen minor variations. No one will, for example, 'thrust' and 'organise' in the same way and the profiles are written to reflect these differences. Some Thruster-Organisers are more outgoing and practically-oriented whereas others are quieter and perhaps more creative. However, both of them will exhibit a high degree of analysis and concern for establishing a well-organised structural approach to the job. All of these differences need to be reflected in the profiles.

After working with many managers and team members we have been able to identify the major ways in which people actually do prefer to do their jobs. Therefore the profiles are written in such a manner as to account for many of these differences. If two people, however, score the Team Management Index in the same way they will receive the same profile description, although they will in actual practice act in their own way and style. Their overall pattern of preference, though, will be the same.

A further point of note is that people with a strong score on the creative dimension of information-gathering may not necessarily end up with a Creator-Innovator profile. The end result of mapping on to the Team Management Wheel very much depends on the interaction of scores on all four work preference constructs. For example, a high score on the creative dimension combined with scores leaning towards introversion, analytical decision-making and structured organisation will result in a Thruster-Organiser major profile. In short, the combination of the various work preferences, rather than one specific factor, goes towards identifying a person's key role preference strengths.

Team development and personal profiles

We have given in this chapter an overview of how the technology for providing feedback to managers and their teams has been created. Further more detailed information for those interested in the research statistics is given in Chapter 9 on Research Data.

In summary, our 'teamwork technology' involves:

- a set of team management roles
- their development into a cognitive managerial map called the Team Management Wheel
- the development of an instrument – the Team Management Index (TMI) – to reliably measure work preferences and team roles
- the writing of a computer program to interpret TMI scores
- the provision of personal profiles (currently 208 in number), each one around 4000 words in length.

These five elements have enabled us to create the basis for systematic team management. We shall describe later the way this is done in such areas as:

- team-building
- team leadership
- work and role allocation
- recruitment and selection
- career planning.

There are many other applications but these are the main ones we shall concentrate on in the remainder of this book.

4

BALANCED TEAMS

When managers are selected to run organisations the first thing they should do is look at the team they have. The team is critical to the achievement of objectives. They can have the right technology, the right finance, and the right market but unless they also have the right management team then they are bound to 'lose'.

Lee Iacocca (Iacocca, 1986) of the Chrysler Motor Company says in his autobiography:

> During the first couple of weeks in a new job, you look for telltale signs. You want to know what kind of fraternity you have joined.

What he found disturbed him. He says, 'Everyone worked independently.'

As he got to know the company he realised that their business and financial problems were to a large extent a result of their lack of teamwork. He goes on to say: 'All of Chrysler's problems really boiled down to the same thing. Nobody knew who was on first.

There was no team, only a collection of independent players, many of whom hadn't yet mastered their positions.'

It was this key organisational problem that he set out to resolve as it was the basis for the long-term improvement of the organisation.

The Disney team

In the Disney partnership it was Walt who was the major Explorer. He was full of ideas which led him to develop such great cartoon films as Snow White and the Seven Dwarfs, Fantasia, Pinocchio, Bambi, and many others. Working alongside him was his brother Roy, who spent a considerable amount of time controlling and organising the business. His job was to identify how much money had been spent on particular projects and to ensure that further revenue was generated and allocated. He was prepared to back his brother's artistic and creative genius even to the extent that, with the Snow White film, they both put everything they had into the film and spent $1.3 million 'on the blind chance of surviving and getting a return on it'.

Invariably, Walt Disney's ideas ran ahead of the money and the organisational arrangements. It wasn't until later in his life that his ideas gained the widespread support that would ensure success.

The differences between Walt and Roy Disney illustrate what it takes to get a successful business off the ground. Teamwork is essential and requires different people playing different roles. The person who is good at one particular aspect of work may well be very poor at another aspect. For example, Roy Disney said of his brother:

Success is hard to take. Walt had moved with his creative talent on his own bent. Business was a damned nuisance to him. After Snow White he wanted to make two animated features a year. We couldn't sustain it. Every creative fellow is so concentrated he does not like to think through the market. Walt was

[37]

that kind of guy until he learned his lesson. Afterwards he became very conscious of market studies. He learned fast.

It was, therefore, through experience that Walt Disney began to realise the need for a wider approach to teamwork and the need to bring in different skills. Initially he was so caught up in his own ideas that he believed they would win through themselves. It was only when he ran into difficulty and people did not support his projects that he began to bring into the team other people who could do the market research and assess the business viability of his ideas.

It is clear that Roy was more the 'Controller', although he clearly had difficulty keeping his brother's imagination in line with the practical realities of the business details. Walt, the 'Explorer', saw the big vision of what could be. Roy saw the detail of what 'is'. Nevertheless, they learned and began to work together well.

In our own research we have been able to quantify what Walt Disney and others have found through experience. If a team is to be successful two ideal conditions have to be met:

- the team must be well balanced with respect to role preferences on the Team Management Wheel
- the team must be well linked.

In this chapter we will deal with the necessary condition of balance. The necessary *and* sufficient condition of 'linking' is discussed in detail in the next chapter.

Procter and Gamble case

John Smale (Smale, 1985) of Procter and Gamble also recognises the importance of getting the right people on a team. He says:

The [Duncan Hines Cookies] team was made up of people from product development, engineering, manufacturing, purchasing, finance and marketing – a multidisciplinary team. But this approach is not an elegant organisational system. It's almost ad hoc in its nature. It's a concept as opposed to a formalised organisational structure. Business teams can be made up of people from all levels of the organisation.... It's a concept that says, 'When you're going to address a problem, get the people who have something to contribute in the way of creativity, if not direct responsibility. Get them together and form that team.' We go out of our way to applaud creativity when we see it, to recognise the people who have made a distinctive contribution.

John Smale says that we must draw on a variety of different people with different strengths if the team is to be strong, as a whole. However, it is not enough to be simply multidisciplinary; the team must also be multi-preference. This is typical of successful teams in 'high-tech' businesses. The high-performing ones are the multi-disciplinary, multi-preference teams.

Interestingly, teams which are multi-disciplinary are often multi-preference also. Concluder-Producers are often attracted into the production or administration disciplines, Creator-Innovators into R & D, Thruster-Organisers into selling, Reporter-Advisers into training and so on. Hence the selection of a multi-disciplinary team often leads to the natural selection of a multi-preference team. However, it is always necessary to check the work preference balance in the team and take appropriate action as necessary.

We have often found that people with a 'Controller-Inspector' or 'Concluder-Producer' preference are attracted into the detail professions such as accounting or operational engineering and feel uncomfortable if they have to work in 'Explorer-Promoter' jobs for any length of time.

People with a preference for 'Reporter-Adviser' or 'Upholder-Maintainer' jobs will often seek out staff-type positions where they are working on their own or in small groups. Usually they avoid conflict situations and prefer not to be involved in activities with a high 'organising' component where hard decisions have to be made quickly. 'Creator-Innovator' people often seek out research and development work where they can play with ideas in an open framework. Their interest and motivation are often associated with new ways of doing things but usually they don't want to be bothered carrying their ideas through to completion.

Since all the team roles defined are important to the success of teamwork, the most successful teams are those composed of members who, between them, are comfortable working in all eight sectors of the Team Management Wheel as well as the 'linker' role. In other words, successful teams are multi-preference teams.

We have worked with many teams that are not multipreference and invariably they run into difficulties, unless they are aware of their weakness and take corrective action.

The computer company team

Not so long ago we experienced an interesting case of management 'defensive play'. A computer company in the retail market had established a firm market base at a time when computers were fairly new and there was little competition. The top team was heavily concentrated in the 'Controlling' section of the wheel and had established an exceptionally efficient system of inventory control and reordering. They knew exactly where each item of stock was and what the profitability was each week. The board was composed of quieter, down-to-earth people whose natural preference led them to adopt 'defensive' play.

They saw the way to improved profit through even further stringencies and cost reductions. However, as more computers came on the market and the 16-bit and 32-bit processors became readily available, computers were coming on the market as 'breakthroughs' and disappearing as 'obsolete' only six months later. Rather than adapt to the exciting changes and the potential for new unheard-of applications, they took a conservative approach and were soon swamped by new companies headed up by 'Exploring' types.

Teams such as this which were weighted into one part of the Team Management Wheel (in this case the 'Controlling' part) often suffer from 'group-think'. Everyone on the team sees the world in the same way and they cosily make decisions which are constrained by their 'model of the world'. These teams are often easy to link together as everyone agrees with the course of action, but usually their lack of 'Exploring' ability causes the team to fail.

Teams which are multi-preference will contain people from all round the Team Management Wheel and this will lead to multiple descriptions of events rather than single descriptions which are more likely when everyone is congregated in one section of the Wheel. However, when multiple descriptions are present then conflict will be incipient and therefore 'linking' is often more difficult.

Architect teams

Partnerships of two or three people working together are also interesting to observe. Dick McCann had major renovations to his house and used a team of two architects to design and document the changes. One of the architects was a model Creative-Innovator, quiet, creative and sometimes with his 'head in the clouds'. His speciality was creative design, the relationships of form and colours. He did not, however, enjoy the detailing and drawing side as much and found it sometimes difficult to spend long hours working on intricate measurements.

Recognising this, he had found a Controller-Inspector to work with – another architect who really enjoyed making sure that every detail was correct and that all specifications were drawn up to be unambiguous to the builder. Together they made a top-class team, but alone they would have been far less successful.

Management games

For several years we used to run a business game at our local University Executive Development Program. This game was run over an eight-hour period with four or five teams competing against each other in a defined market place. When assigning people to teams we would usually take all the Thruster-Organisers and put them into the one team. We would then form two teams that were reasonably well balanced and the last team would usually contain 'left Wheel' people (Creator-Innovators, Reporter-Advisers and Upholder-Maintainers).

Over the four years we ran this game the Thruster-Organisers always finished last and one of the balanced teams usually won the game. One or two Thruster-Organisers in a team is great, but as more are added they become very competitive and start pulling in different directions. They will often argue loudly and engage in a lot of 'parallel conversation', where words float by in unconnected parallel streams.

Teams of 'left Wheel' people show different dynamics, but they too have their problems. In the management game they would usually work cooperatively and with enthusiasm but they always failed to work in a systematic manner, focusing on the outputs required in the game. As a result they never allowed enough time for their decisions and often had to make a hurried 'decision by vote' in the last seconds of each time period.

Working together

When team members understand the different work preferences or 'frames of reference' that people have then excellent teamwork can result. Thruster-Organisers, for example, are people who often need to work with Reporter-Advisers or Upholder-Maintainers. However, because their ways of working are very different, both parties need to make allowances and use their linking skills.

Thruster-Organisers are anxious to make decisions, to get into action, and sometimes they can't be bothered to gather the information required. It is here that many successful Thruster-Organisers have learned to cooperate with people on the left side of the Wheel. Chairmen have their advisers (probably people on the left side of the Wheel) and company CEOs usually rely on their staff function or their corporate planning department to provide them with important information concerning mergers, acquisitions and take-overs.

Explorer-Promoters often benefit from an association with a Controller-Inspector. Explorer-Promoters are usually outgoing and often work with several different ideas or projects simultaneously. Typically they have many balls in the air and if they are not careful the balls will all crash to the ground. Therefore they often need Controller-Inspectors around them to 'pick up the pieces'.

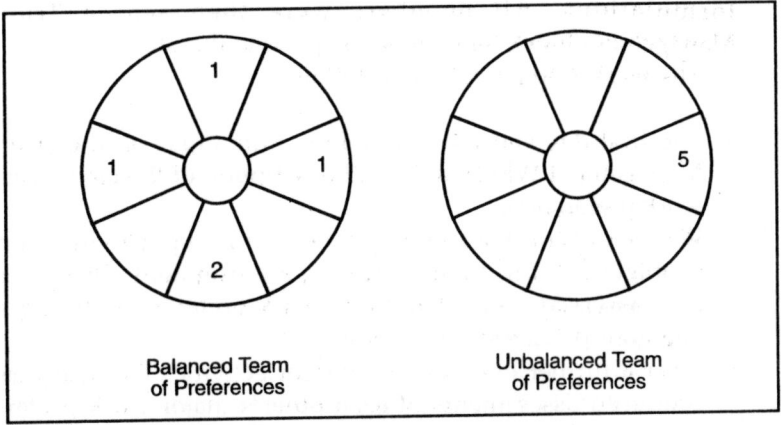

Balanced Team
of Preferences

Unbalanced Team
of Preferences

Figure 5.

Unigate Dairies

Terry Mills, Group Training Manager of St Ivel Ltd, has used the Team Management Wheel to develop executive teams in Unigate Dairies (a subsidiary of St Ivel Ltd). He reports:

Team Management

A General Manager and his executive team, faced with a changing market place (i.e. movements in customer buying patterns and price competition), decided they needed to formulate a new strategy which would increase sales penetration within their existing customer base and exploit all opportunities to attract new customers.

This team of six, including three new members, agreed that they would all benefit from a team development activity. They wanted to accelerate their ability to function as a more integrated team and hence be more likely to achieve their (yet to be agreed) strategy.

The Team Management Wheel, introduced by myself, was chosen as the vehicle around which to build a four-day workshop. Discussions were held with the General Manager and we agreed on overall objectives for the team-building and strategy formulations. All members were then sent a Team Management Index for completion prior to the programme.

The workshop proceeded as follows:

- The first day started with a 45-minute input on the Team Management Wheel and a full description of the eight basic work preferences.
- We then spent one-and-a-half days on group activities and problem-solving in an outdoors environment. Delegates then assessed their own major work preferences during a one-hour private study session.
- After a further one day on outdoor activities the delegates produced assessments of each other's major work preferences and shared their views in a short group session.
- Scored profiles were then issued to individuals.
- Profiles were then discussed in pairs to provide feedback on how they perceived each other.
- The overall team balance was then checked against the Wheel and action plans agreed to ensure that missing work preferences were exercised in future group decision-making discussions.

[44]

- The final evening and following day were then spent on strategy formulation with frequent reviews to ensure that all work preferences were being utilised.

As a result of this workshop a practical strategy statement and associated tactics were drawn up to which all team members were enthusiastically committed and which were underpinned by a comprehensive understanding of how a high-performing team operates.

Terry, in his intervention, enabled the team members to understand 'differences' and showed them the importance of achieving team balance so that all roles on the Team Management Wheel were effectively covered.

How to balance the team

Some teams will be able to correct imbalances by moving people elsewhere in the organisation and bringing in people to plug the gaps. However, this is not always possible, because groups are sometimes put together on an ad hoc basis and there is no freedom of choice for team members. Therefore the group may be heavily weighted on one side of the Wheel or another. In these cases it is important to realise the potential weakness of the group and, if possible, take some corrective action. Two solutions that managers have come up with are worth mentioning:

The factory team

We were working with a factory team whose members mapped into the Thruster-Organiser, Concluder-Producer and Controller-Inspector roles. They agreed that they needed more emphasis in the areas of 'Exploring' and 'Advising'. They had a long discussion on what to do about it. As a result, they decided to have a workshop and spend time operating in the Creator-Innovator

[45]

sector of the Team Management Wheel. They hired a creative consultant who could introduce some new perspectives into their view of the workplace. They had an enlightening two days. As a result, they agreed to repeat the exercise regularly on an annual basis and to make more use of consultants, who often bring in a fresh way of looking at things.

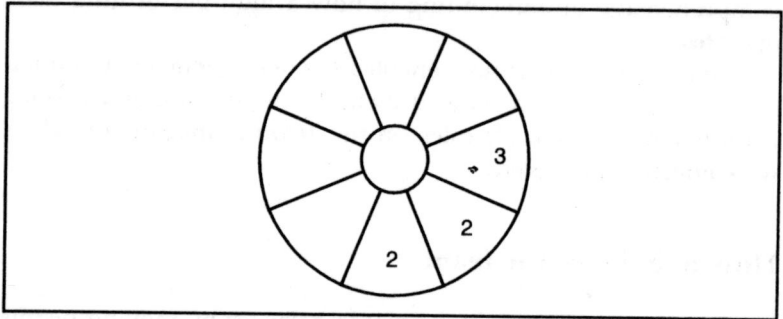

Figure 6. Factory Team work preferences.

Thus they were able to balance the Team Management Wheel in two ways:

1 They forced themselves to make a journey over to the Creator-Innovator part of the Wheel, an area which was foreign to their preference. Therefore they needed the support of an experienced facilitator skilled in running creative meetings. In this way innate creativity was harnessed and some fundamental new perspectives introduced.

2 Consultants invariably have a preference for the 'Advising-Exploring' quadrant of the Team Management Wheel. By hiring them on a regular basis, they can be used to balance the team. Thruster-Organisers, Concluder-producers and Controller-Inspectors may not want them around permanently, but they can certainly benefit from regular interaction with them.

The sales team

A sales team in a large organisation was composed of a sales manager and his regional representatives who all mapped into the Explorer-Promoter, Assessor-Developer and Thruster-Organiser sectors of the Team Management Wheel. Upon discussing the results, they seemed pleased that they were all in this upper quadrant of the Team Management Wheel. When it was pointed out that there were no 'Controllers' in the team, they said that they didn't need them because that function was carried out by central administration. They were asked how often they met with central administration and they simultaneously answered 'Never'. It was then realised that their real team was a wider one that should include representatives from the control side of the organisation. After much discussion, they agreed and arranged to invite the Administration Manager to their meetings. This was the start of a new era of cooperation between two parts of an organisation that traditionally had a 'them' and 'us' view of each other.

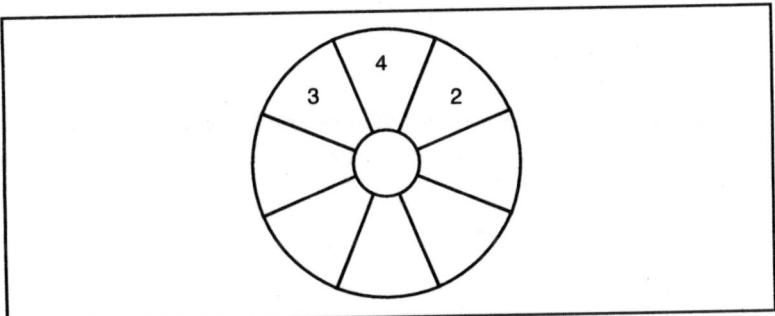

Figure 7. Sales Team work preferences.

In our own Team Management Systems team we are very 'top heavy' with five people in the Creator-Innovator, Explorer-Promoter and Assessor-Developer sectors. Our Assessor-Developer, however, can move himself easily into the Concluder-Producer sector and help out when it comes to getting a job finished. Likewise we have another person whose main preference is the Explorer-Promoter area but who contributes well in the Thruster-Organiser role when required. In balancing your team, therefore, the first thing to do is to identify the gaps and then discuss how various people might 'stretch themselves' so that all eight outer sectors of the Team Management Wheel are covered.

Another team we worked with was very successful in coming up with new products and services and selling them, but they continually had problems in keeping their records straight. Frequently there were cash flow problems caused by too rapid a growth in the business. Expenditure was overcommitted and did not match expected revenue. However, they felt they were too small to have a full-time person in the Controller-Inspector role. We therefore suggested they get someone on a part-time basis in that role. Since then they have been more effective and the talents of the Creator-Innovators and Explorer-Promoters have been released to do what they do best, rather than worrying over the systems and procedures.

Teamwork review

Consider now your own team. Where are the key strengths? Are you a team primarily of Advisers, or Explorers, or Organisers or Controllers?

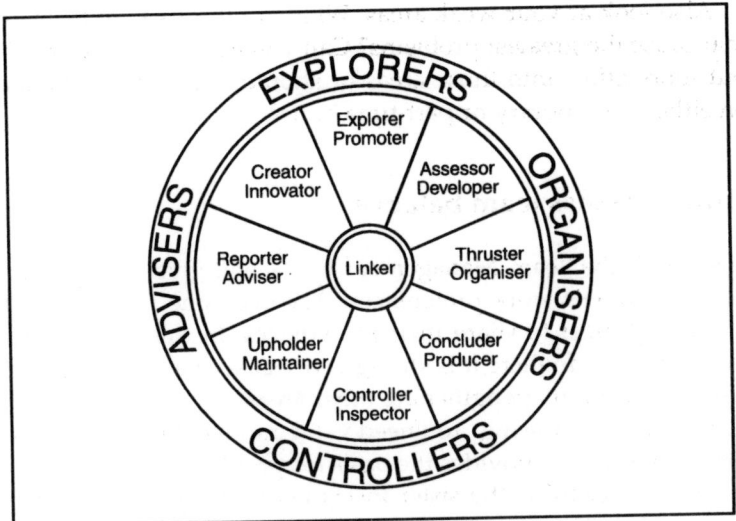

Figure 8. The Margerison-McCann Team Management Wheel.

Team Members   Team Role

_____   _____
_____   _____
_____   _____
_____   _____
_____   _____
_____   _____
_____   _____

My team has gaps in the following areas:
_____
_____
_____

I will balance the team by:
_____
_____
_____
_____

[49]

Also look at your weak areas. What are the areas of teamwork that cause the greatest problems? Can you get one of your team to put more effort into those areas or should you appoint someone on either a temporary or part-time basis?

How to assess team balance

First of all the Team Management Index will give you an indication of people's work preferences. Ask everyone to complete the Index and meet to share their preferences. In this way the team can understand where it is strong and weak. They can also decide what to do about strengthening other areas.

It is no use guessing. You need valid and reliable data. The TMI can do this and it provides the basis for problem-solving.

Equally useful is the sister instrument, the Team Performance Index (TPI). This enables the team to gain a 360° view of their efforts from their customers, colleague groups, superiors and others with whom they interact. This feedback provides detailed and quantitative answers as well as written information on how team members see their performance compared to others.

It is the group as well as personal feedback that can make the difference to discussions on how a team should organise itself. Working on data is better than everyone guessing and swapping individual prejudices. Increasingly teams are therefore using instruments to enhance their reporting and advising before they thrust and organise.

5

QUALITY TEAMWORK

The word quality has become central to modern business. It is no use just producing products and services – they have to reflect quality. The use of the Team Management Wheel has been important in helping define what quality means between people at work.

As Alan Barratt, who was a Management Development Manager for Mobil and is now an international consultant, said: 'What I like about the Team Wheel Model is that it provides a basis to assess different aspects of quality – and in particular quality teamwork.'

This is true, because without quality teamwork the other functional aspects of quality will begin to break down. However, by looking at nine major work functions a team – and an individual also – can assess performance quality in each of the areas. To help facilitate this we developed the Team Performance Index. This is a sister instrument to the Personal Team Management Index and the Types of Work Index, but concentrates on the team as a whole.

The Team Performance Index, as it is called, enables any team to gain feedback on how its members see their performance in the nine areas of the Types of Work Wheel. Also those with whom the team interacts can provide feedback on the team's performance, as shown in Figure 9.

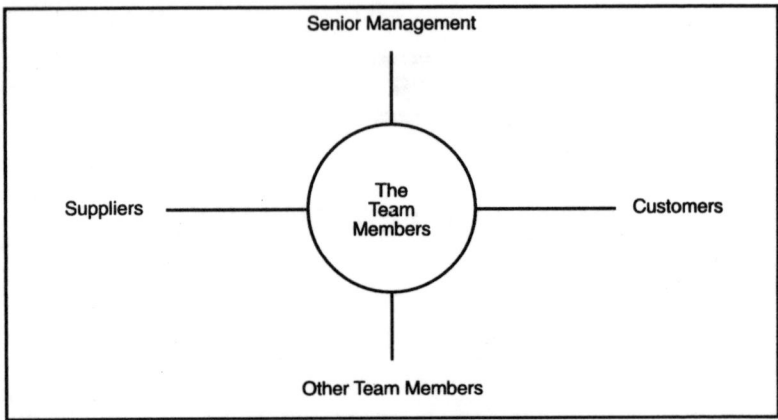

Figure 9. Team Performance Index.

The opportunity to gather and use this valuable information is called 360° feedback in that it gives an all round view of the team's performance. The TPI has similar items to the TWI but focussed on how the team operates rather than defining the job. The result is that:

- team members can rate the team.
- the customers can rate the team.
- the suppliers can rate the team.
- the members of other colleague teams can also provide a rating.

Software has been developed to provide an easy-to-use work-orientated feedback. An example of this is shown below.

QUALITY TEAMWORK

Types of Work Satisfaction Rates

Types of Work	Satisfaction Rate %	Importance Rating %	Ranking
Advising		85	5
Team Average	83		
JB001	96		
JS002	82		
HB003	100		
SG004	72		
BL005	83		
Advising		69	9
Team Average	90		
JB001	94		
JS002	100		
HB003	100		
SG004	78		
BL005	90		
Innovating		74	8
Team Average	95		
JB001	96		
JS002	94		
HB003	100		
SG004	96		
BL005	94		
Developing		76	7
Team Average	89		
JB001	100		
JS002	96		
HB003	100		
SG004	68		
BL005	78		
Organising		85	6
Team Average	90		
JB001	96		
JS002	100		
HB003	100		
SG004	72		
BL005	72		
Producing		97	2
Team Average	98		
JB001	96		
JS002	100		
HB003	100		
SG004	100		
BL005	94		
Inspecting		96	3
Team Average	100		
JB001	100		
JS002	100		
HB003	100		
SG004	100		
BL005	100		
Maintaining		98	1
Team Average	100		
JB001	100		
JS002	100		
HB003	100		
SG004	100		
BL005	100		
Linking		91	4
Team Average	84		
JB001	81		
JS002	83		
HB003	76		
SG004	90		
BL005	90		

[53]

The value of this kind of data is that it provides a quick visual guide on differences. These form the basis for discussion by the team members on what needs to be done in order to improve. Where there are major gaps between the perceptions, we therefore recommend that face-to-face discussions take place to clarify what is meant and agree what has to be done. This can involve the following:

- Team differences – sometimes the main differences are between team members themselves. Some team members, for example, may rate the team's performance on Innovating and Promoting as low, while others may assess the team to be strong in the Inspecting areas. Now it is vital that the members meet to (a) define what they mean, (b) give examples, (c) develop options for improvement, and (d) agree on a line of action.

- Inter-team differences – when members of other teams provide data which differs from the perceptions of the team members this is clearly a time to review. If a customer rates the team performance on Advising as low and the team sees it as acceptable then discussions need to take place. It is best if this is done face to face. Indeed the value of any instrument such as the TPI is only as good as the discussion and problem-solving it helps generate.

Quality and teamwork

The above processes should help define what quality means as far as customers, colleagues, clients and the team itself is concerned. Too often the word quality means many things to many people. Like Humpty Dumpty in Alice in Wonderland, who said 'When I use a word it means exactly what I mean it to mean', the word Quality does not in such circumstances mean very much. It is only through discussion and agreement on what others require that we can enhance quality standards.

It is in this context that the Types of Work Wheel provides a tremendous guide to quality improvement. The team should be able to list and measure what it will do to make continuous improvements in the key nine areas of The Margerison-McCann Types of Work Wheel. For example, the following is a partial listing of the points identified by one team on the work functions:

Advising   Identify the quantity and quality of current reports in conjunction with stakeholders and set goals for service levels.

Innovating   Review innovations that have occurred over the past 12 months and identify areas for consideration and experimentation in the next 12 months.

Promoting   Listen to customers on current promotions and adjust the quantity and quality in light of feedback.

Developing   Assess the effectiveness of new developments over the last 12 months and set priorities and targets for the next period in conjunction with other complementary groups.

Organising   Work out the way resources have been employed and look for specific restructuring to meet the needs of the tasks.

Producing   An audit of outputs and consideration of operational procedures to ensure delivery.

Inspecting   A review of procedures and involvement of users in the redesign of what needs to be done.

Maintaining   A reassessment of the standards and their implementation and introduction of new levels of quality to further the improvement process.

[55]

Team Management

Linking   To consider feedback from stakeholders on the communication and linking process and adapt specific campaigns to improve performance.

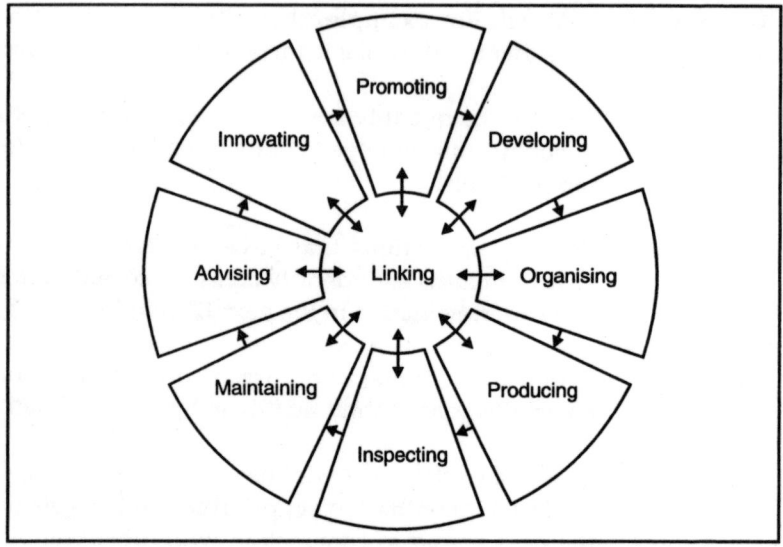

Figure 10. The Margerison-McCann Types of Work Model.

A team or individual can therefore look at its performance quality in nine relevant ways by asking 'what quality levels do we have on each of the work functions – and do we meet them?' A straight forward exercise is to enquire:

- What is quality Advice?
- What is quality Innovation?
- What is quality Promotion?
- What is quality Development?
- What is quality Organisation?
- What is quality Production?
- What is quality Inspection?
- What is quality Maintenance?
- What is quality Linking?

This provides a simple, relevant work-based approach to quality assessment.

Example – Case A

A team who used this approach to define its quality success areas realised that it was not devoting sufficient thought or time to Advising, Innovating and Promoting. As the manager said, 'We focus mainly on keeping the existing system working well. We have good standards for what we produce. We are organised, but we don't come up with new ways of doing things.'

We arranged for his team to gain feedback via the TPI. As a result the team discussed how they should develop themselves to improve their Advising, Innovating and Promoting. This involved more time being spent on these activities in workshops and more experimental projects. The result was an increase in new ideas for product development, improved problem-solving data and better presentations by those involved.

Case B

Another business team was very interested in seeing how others perceived their performance. They therefore completed the TPI and also asked customers, colleagues and senior managers to provide their views. To facilitate discussion we produced a matrix for team development, as shown over the page.

This led to in-depth discussions on how the team could improve its quality in areas of importance to the groups with whom it interacted. In particular, they focused on the areas where there were gaps between the teams views and those of others. Discussions were held with customers on what extra information and advice they needed and also their production requirements. With other colleagues the discussion centred on how they could improve their inter-group links and coordination and also work closer on projects and product development. With their supervisor the team concentrated on an overall review of the teamwork functions and specific action plans for improvement.

	TEAM VIEW	CUSTOMERS' VIEW	COLLEAGUES' VIEW	SUPERVISORS' VIEW
ADVISING	High	Low	Medium	High
INNOVATING	Low	Medium	Low	Medium
PROMOTING	Medium	High	Medium	Medium
DEVELOPING	High	Medium	Low	Medium
ORGANISING	High	High	Medium	High
PRODUCING	High	Low	Medium	Medium
INSPECTING	Medium	Low	High	Low
MAINTAINING	Medium	Low	Medium	High
LINKING	High	Medium	Low	High

Areas for teamwork development.

The whole process took a few months as meetings had to be fixed and the time allocated to work on the issues raised. As one member of the group said, 'It was hard work but very worth-while. We established a clearer focus for our efforts and better relationships between ourselves and our colleagues and clients.'

There are no quick fixes in teamwork but gathering relevant data and discussing it with those who can have an influence is a vital and relevant approach to take. The Team Performance Index facilitates this and generates a professional problem-solving approach.

Summary

The Margerison-McCann Types of Work Wheel has been useful in helping teams define what quality teamwork means and working with their stakeholders to agree improvement. The Team Performance Index, in association with the other TMS instruments, is helpful to provide the data to facilitate the discussions. It is after all the quality discussion that produces the basis for improvement. If quality is to be enhanced a key starting point is to ensure you have quality teamwork.

6

LINKING SKILLS FOR SUCCESS

Everyone has a different way of performing their job but the really successful people are those who can claim to be 'team linkers'.

'Linking' is at the centre of the Team Management Wheel and is a skill that team members can learn. It is important to note that 'linking' is not a preference but a skill. Therefore as a team member you will have a preference for one or more of the sectors of the Team Management Wheel, but if you can also hold the centre space as a 'linker' then you will be well on the road to contributing to a high-performing team.

Achieving a balance in terms of preferences means that people with different 'models of reality' will be constantly interacting. These differences will create a diversity of views and this can lead to better decisions and prevent 'group-think'. However, diversity may create conflict and therefore well-balanced teams will not always be 'high-performing'. We have seen beautifully balanced teams fail because there was no 'linking' being done. People talked behind others' backs, there was no cooperation or exchange of ideas and the meetings often degenerated into slanging matches. 'Linking', therefore, is the second essential condition required for high performance in teams.

There are three different types of linking that we have observed in teams: internal linking, external linking and informal linking.

Internal linking – coordinating

Every manager, it is generally agreed, has to get work done 'through people'. Those who are more successful at this are usually skilled 'internal linkers'. They have not only been able to allocate work to members of the team and give guidance and direction on goals to be obtained, but have enabled the members to work together in a cooperative way. It is this last point which is often the difference between individual effort and effective team-work.

In the course of our research we studied hundreds of managers and looked closely at the various strategies they employed for linking the team into an effective unit. In all cases there was a clearly thought-out approach that enabled people to cooperate and work together as a team. Much of the managers' time was given over to what we have called 'internal linking' — a process of ensuring that all members of the team are coordinated and integrated towards a common goal.

Figure 11 shows some examples of good and bad internal linking. In the first diagram the manager has established good links between himself and the rest of the team, but the links between team members are virtually non-existent. The managerial style of the leader of a team like this would be to have everyone coming to him whenever there were problems. Most likely all decisions would have to pass through him and as a result he is likely to be under considerable pressure. In the second example there is good internal linking where robust links have been established between team members as well as through the leader. A team which is managed in this way is strongly linked together and is more likely to act as a 'unit' rather than as a collection of individuals.

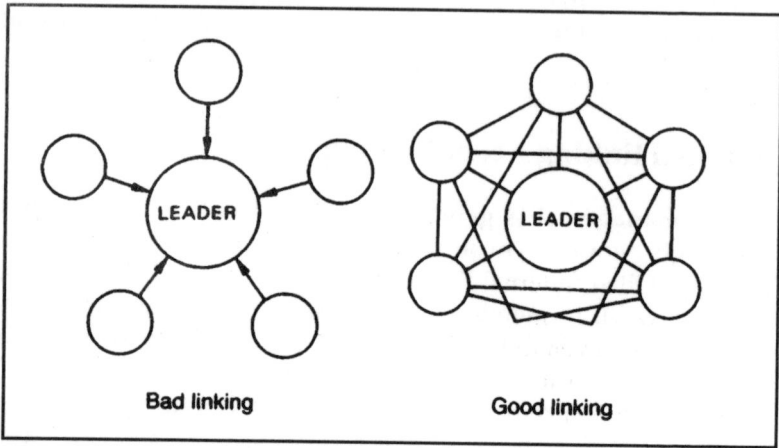

Figure 11. Examples of good and bad internal linking.

In some cases up to 80 per cent of the team leader's time might need to be devoted to linking. Managers should realise this and define their role in such a way that they have plenty of time to practise their linking skills. This is a common mistake that young managers make. When promoted they often try to retain much of the technical content of their work and their time spent on 'linking' is very low. As a result they often work long hours and end up with team outputs that are well below optimum.

However, it is not just the manager who has to link. All team members have responsibility for linking well with others. Being a good internal linker is not easy. It requires a conscious decision by team members.

External linking – representing

As a vital element of being a team leader, it is necessary that managers act as representatives of their team. In this task they are also playing a most important part as an 'external linker'.

Each team needs effective members who can represent team members both upwards and laterally. Managers have to be effective advocates of what their team requires by way of resources so that the tasks can be achieved optimally. They also need to promote both the individual and group efforts to those people in the organisation who have wider influence. However, other team members act as external linkers on projects and committees.

Equally, managers need to be good representatives of their team when working with colleagues at the same level, say from different departments or divisions. Here the issues are more likely to involve the resolution of interdepartmental problems and ensuring that fairness and equity prevail. To stay in business it is rare for one department or division to be able to do its job adequately without cooperation from other units and therefore the role of the manager as an external lateral linker is of increasing importance and demands particular skills in problem-solving and communication.

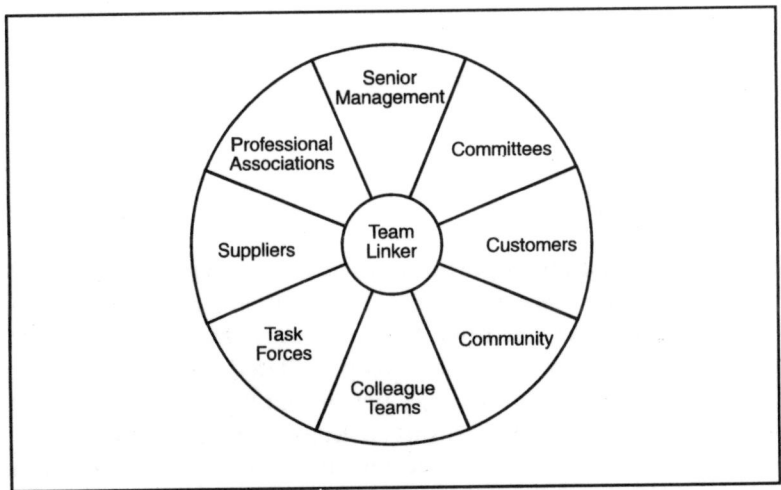

Figure 12.

External linking is a special case of interface management. As we move towards the year 2000 the role of a manager is becoming increasingly a representative. The success of a team can often depend on other teams both within the organisation and outside. Therefore one of the key skills of the external linker is to identify the key interfaces that impact upon the success of the team and to spend time in managing these interfaces (see figure 12).

Informal linking

Internal and external linking are formal roles which should be undertaken by the team leader. In addition to these there is also another class of linking which can be done by all team members. This is known as informal linking. All team members can contribute to the establishment of links within their team and also make individual contributions towards developing external links. If all team members contribute to informal linking then the team will be so strongly bound together that it becomes resilient to 'attacks'. This is all part of what is called networking to discover what is going on and having contacts to deal with problems and opportunities as they arise.

Linkers in action

We have now had the opportunity to observe and study a number of managers who were deemed by their staff and colleagues to be effective linkers. We identified these managers from comments by their own team members. These people offered unsolicited praise of the way the managers actually performed their jobs. Given that people do not normally go out of their way to praise others, particularly their managers, we felt that the people in question were probably applying certain principles in a way that was not only acceptable but functional for getting the job done. It is easy to become well liked by doing things which please people, but not always so easy to get the job done on time to given standards and still be appreciated.

One manager we studied was Jim Lewis. In a series of interviews we conducted within his organisation, typical comments made were as follows.

- 'Although Jim is an accountant and not an expert in the technology of the industry, he is actually very good at getting all the technical people to work together.'
- 'I work very closely with Jim Lewis and I have a lot of respect for the time he takes to listen to what people have to say. He looks for practical approaches to solving problems which will meet people's individual needs, but without diluting the best answer for the organisation as a whole.'
- 'I am an engineer by background and I did not believe that Jim Lewis would be able to get this team to work together. I have to admit, though, that the way he brings us together in various meetings and gets the information out so that decisions are made is an improvement over what had happened before.'
- 'Managers like Jim Lewis have a difficult job because they have to continually satisfy head office while at the same time keeping together their own team of highly technical professional people. I always feel he makes a good job at both ends by representing our interest at head office and at the same time putting across to us what they are trying to achieve. In this way we can at least see the wider situation even if we don't always agree with it.'

None of these comments in themselves told us what Lewis was doing to gain respect from his team members. We had to look more closely at the day-to-day operations and the ideas underlying his approach to management. In this we found he applied key issues which are characteristic of effective managerial linkers.

Key aspects of how linkers work

In our research with various organisations in a variety of industries we have been able to identify some of the key points that
people continually refer to when they talk about effective
managerial behaviour. In looking at these descriptions of actual
behaviour it was quite clear that effective managers were seen by
other people to be skilled at holding people together while at the
same time driving forward towards the achievement of objectives.
They were good therefore not only at linking people together as a
social unit, but also at linking them towards achieving the task
output.

The managers spent an enormous amount of time, not so much
in doing any specific technical job but in coordinating and integrating the work of others. We therefore coined the term 'linker'
to explain what they were doing. From our studies we identified
11 key linking skills that encompass internal linking, external
linking and informal linking. These 11 skills are:

1 Active listening.
2 Communication.
3 Problem-solving and counselling.
4 Team development.
5 Work allocation.
6 Team relationships
7 Delegation.
8 Quality standards.
9 Objectives setting.
10 Interface management.
11 Participative decision-making.

We shall now discuss these in more detail using Jim Lewis as an
example, where appropriate. They can, however, be measured by
the Linking Skills Index, a 66-item questionnaire. It enables you to
gain feedback from your colleagues and boss as well as yourself
on the 11 key areas.

The application of the principles in practice

1 Active listening

It is usually said of people who are effective that they are able to understand other people's views. What this really means in practice is that the individuals who are expressing a point of view feel that the other person actually does understand what they have said. In this case Jim Lewis was very effective in his listening skills. He knew when to talk and when to listen. In particular he was good at summarising the views and concerns of other people. However, beyond that he would pick up the key points and indicate that even if he could not do anything immediately, he would work on the problems raised and report back.

This was echoed by another manager who said, 'One of the characteristics of working in this team is that there are lots of opportunities for people to put their views before decisions are made. If anything, I would probably criticise the team for having too many meetings. However, Jim Lewis believes that it is important that everyone should be committed before we make decisions and this is certainly reflected in the way in which we work.'

These points of view are good illustrations of the way team members feel when managers take time to listen and understand.

'Listening' is one of the key skills of communication. Further information on the role of the linker as a communicator and influencer is given in the books *How to Influence Others at Work* by Dick McCann and *If Only I Had Said* by Charles Margerison.

2 Communication

'What we have here are lots of meetings. Some people would say that we have too many. However, no one can say that people don't understand what is going on,' said one member of Jim Lewis's team. Another member of the team said, 'A lot of the back-biting and arguments that used to go on under the previous manager no longer seem to occur, although all the members of the team are the same. I can only put this down to the fact that we now have more regular meetings and a wider base for understanding each other's work. This is very much a characteristic of Jim Lewis's approach to management.'

Indeed Lewis put a tremendous emphasis upon the importance of meetings and getting work done in an atmosphere where people could keep up to date, not only by hearing what he had to say but by listening to what others had to say. In essence he had five major meetings in which he sought to bring about team understanding. These were the weekly technical meeting, the fortnightly management meeting, the three-monthly general staff business communication meeting, the personal individual meetings, and the departmental monthly report meetings. In addition there were a number of other forums which Jim Lewis had for keeping contact, such as task-force briefings, but these were the main ways in which he sought to keep others up to date on a regular basis, as well as to brief himself. 'Although it takes a long time to be involved in such meetings,' said Jim Lewis, 'it pays off in terms of getting people to work together effectively. My job is not to do any technical work at all but simply to ensure that the team is working to its maximum potential.'

3 Problem-solving and counselling

Everyone at work from time to time comes up with either personal or work-based problems which they need to talk over with someone. 'Linking' will create an environment where they encourage people to discuss these problems with them. Solutions to the problems are then generated and many managers use these sessions as a way of coaching and developing their staff. When a problem is raised 'linking' managers will usually ask for possible solution options and then work through the solutions showing the team member how to come to the best decision. If the problems are trivial then they will indicate this and direct the team member to a person who might help them.

One of Jim Lewis's team members said, 'Although Jim is extremely busy, I would say that he is willing to talk through particular problems. The one thing I will say for him is that he does have an excellent follow-up system. Although he may not be able to do anything immediately, he does continually work at it and let you know what is happening.'

People who are good at Linking skill No. 3 are not necessarily sitting in their offices every day waiting for people to bring them problems. Indeed in many cases they have conditioned their staff to come in not only with the problem but with possible solutions. However, where there are really difficult personal, emotional or work problems they encourage people to come in and talk them over in an open way. It is this 'conditioning process' which is important and if correctly done will enable people to know the terms under which help will be readily given.

Being 'available' by itself is not sufficient. Linkers must also be 'responsive'. When staff come to see you with a problem, it is probably of major concern to them. It is no good being available to listen if you are not also responsive. Employees often refer to these people as 'mirror managers' – bosses who say 'I'll look into it', and that is the last they ever hear on the matter.

4 Team development

We showed earlier the importance of having a balance in our team. Every team needs people who between them cover the Exploring, Controlling, Advising and Organising sectors of the Team Management Wheel.

These functions are necessary in every organisation. However, very often managers do not have the chance to choose their team members and have to make do with the existing skills and abilities. Effective linkers recognise the strengths of their work team and ensure that time is allocated for all the sectors of the Team Management Wheel.

[69]

Team Management

In the case of Jim Lewis, he recognised that the team was very strong in the 'Controlling' and 'Organising' areas. He felt that more attention could be given to advisory work and exploring new approaches. He therefore reorganised the structure to enable people to spend more time on this kind of work. Often he would run 'brain-storming' sessions where he encouraged people to come up with new ideas regardless of how 'way-out' they might initially seem. Eventually one of his team transferred to another division and Jim set about finding a creative Assessor-Developer for the team.

5 Work allocation

Successful managers who are effective at 'linking' take time out to discuss with individuals what their own preferred approach to work is and try to organise tasks in accordance with people's abilities. Many of them use the normal appraisal processes to do this. Our own work through the use of the Team Management Index has also given individuals the opportunity to make assessments of their own strengths and how they can best contribute to a team.

In the case of Jim Lewis's team it was suggested it might be helpful if they all completed a Team Management Index. This they did and team members received a 4000-word personal profile outlining their own preferences on a number of factors such as decision-making, interpersonal skills, team-building, and various other work-related aspects. Team members found the personal profiles very helpful and decided to share them amongst one another.

This stimulated debate on how the team worked. In particular it focused attention on how team members could help one another to do their job better. In general they felt that as a result of the discussion people would be more able to use their strengths in the work that they did and have more discretion in delegating work in which they themselves were perhaps not so strong.

6 Team relationships

This was one of the most noticeable skills present in all the well-linked teams with which we worked. There was an atmosphere of cooperation rather than conflict.

Team members referred on many occasions to the fact that the team leader worked hard to engender an attitude of goodwill. This was certainly the case in Jim Lewis's team:

> I was a bit cynical about the new approach that Jim Lewis introduced because under the previous manager there had been a lot of inter-departmental rivalry and competition. However, I would say that the atmosphere and the spirit is far better now.
>
> Jim Lewis makes it clear that he's not interested in having people score points off each other and does not set one department against the other. There are still some inter-personal problems as there will be in any organisation, but basically people do try to work well together. I can only put this down to the fact that Jim has made it absolutely clear that he wants cooperation amongst team members to get the job done. He certainly sets an example by showing respect for each person and the work of their particular function, and above all has a genuine interest in what everyone does. I'm sure this carries over to the work of other people. We all feel we can trust one another.

One way of addressing this problem is to get people to talk through their preferences and to share and compare their profiles. Often this causes team members to see one another in a different light and, if correctly managed, new working relationships can be developed. A team without respect, understanding and trust is not a team.

7 Delegation

Top managers are bound to be overloaded. It is therefore vital that they are able to distinguish the important from the urgent. In the case of the linkers we talked with, we found that they spent some time actually having their team members work with them on what the priorities should be. They actually opened up the agenda to the team members and discussed what the priority issues should be, not only for the team but for themselves as the senior manager.

In Jim Lewis's case, he found that he was spending far too much time away from the office, and in discussion with the team they indicated that they needed to be able to communicate with him on a more regular basis. He therefore reorganised his schedule so that he spent less time overseas and brought in another person to handle a lot of the contract and negotiation work. This gave him more time to work with his own team on an individual basis, as well as being able to represent them to head office.

Whereas everyone stressed that delegating is important, we have found that managerial linkers actually identify, usually with their team, the top five things they must concentrate on. They then set up regular ways of reviewing whether these five things are being achieved and develop regular planning schedules to ensure that they are on target.

8 Quality standards

All through our life we look up to people who set a good example. As small children we often want to be just like Mum or Dad when we grow up. When we go to school there is often a teacher we admire – someone we take as a role model for our behaviour. So too is it in the workplace. People will unconsciously seek a role model in the senior management staff. If you can set this good example then people will respect you and want to work hard to achieve the team outputs.

In our research with managers we noted that the favourite topic of conversation in poorly-linked teams was 'the boss'. During coffee breaks or in the lunch hour they were always 'running down the boss'. However, where Linking skill No. 8 was well implemented, then usually positive comments were made rather than negative ones.

Setting an example of quality is also important in achieving high-performing team status. Delivering outputs to 'customers' at the right quality is one way in which the team's performance is measured. Defining this 'quality' and keeping the team up to it is what Linking skill No. 8 is all about.

In our various discussions we found that managerial linkers take time, often away from the normal day-to-day work environment, to look at the wider context in which work is being done. It is easy to get caught up with the facts and figures of today and forget about tomorrow. However, managerial linkers are as much concerned with the long term as the short term. In this regard quality is a very important aspect, not only in terms of the physical factors involved, but also the social factors. We discovered that managerial linkers were able to put time aside for workshops to look at 'How our team is performing in such areas as satisfying customers, developing staff skills, improving product performance, and enhancing the quality of working life.'

Quality standards are all about continuously improving to meet client/customer expectations.

9 Objectives setting

We found that managerial linkers who were doing a good job were not easy people to work for. They were not people who took life easily: they set themselves a fast pace and expected other people to run accordingly. While they would help, support and guide, they ultimately judged people against the outputs that were achieved. Many people we spoke with indicated that the targets set were difficult but attainable, provided the motivation levels were maintained at a high level. In other words, the managerial linker involved people in discussing how the targets should be achieved but also, through experience in judgement, use standards and outputs which required people to stretch. Overall we did not find that people objected to this, provided that they were involved in discussing how those targets and objectives were to be achieved.

Therefore in setting targets for team members it is important to match them to individual abilities. Each person should be stretched, but not assigned targets that are clearly ridiculous. Then they should be encouraged by coaching, counselling and by support not only to achieve the set targets but to go beyond them.

10 Interface management

This skill summarises the key aspects of managing the internal and external interfaces of the team. It covers the coordinating and representing of team members.

Coordinating the team is an internal linking activity and is essential if team members are to pull in the same direction. Representing the team is an external linking activity and is all about influencing other managers external to the team.

'Managing upwards' is an essential external linking technique if team leaders want to get their budgets accepted and get resources – money, equipment, people – to do the job in an efficient and effective manner. Team members will often judge the leader's performance on how good they are at getting resources for the team. In this regard their own rewards in terms of pay and conditions are often uppermost in their minds.

Managers who are good at external linking may be poor at internal linking. Explorer-Promoters are sometimes like this. They can be so busy developing links with external entities that they are never in their office to do any internal linking. As a result the team falls apart. When this occurs there is often the need to delegate the internal linking function to someone else in the team.

11 *Participative decision-making*

Wherever we went we found that managerial linkers had an excellent track record for involving people. As Jim Lewis indicated, there were five main meetings that he established to get information for decisions. However, beyond this, he had a whole range of other areas of activities such as task forces and policy forums to get views, opinions and information in order to press on with the job.

Solutions which are imposed from above have a high failure rate. If you want commitment to the implementation of a solution, the golden rule is to involve those affected at an early stage. Even if you ultimately proceed with your own original ideas, the fact that you have communicated them to the team at an early stage and let them air their views will smooth the way to implementation.

When you impose solutions on others you are the owner of the solution and therefore people may not necessarily give of their best. If, however, you involve them in the problem-solving of key issues, then they become part-owners of the solution and as such win 'go that extra mile' to ensure that the solution is satisfactorily implemented.

The Linking Skills Profile

As a result of the questionnaire we created based on the above listening skills we can now provide detailed feedback to teams and individuals. A sample of one page of a report is given on the next page.

Improving linking skills

Even teams that are well balanced can fail if linking is not carried out to a high standard. Richard Peters realised this when he attended one of our Linking Skills Workshops.

[75]

Team Management

Linking Skills Satisfaction Rates

Linking Skill	Satisfaction Rate %	Importance Rating %	Ranking
01 Active Listening			
Self	82	83	1 (eq)
Co-worker Group A	42	99	3 (eq)
Co-worker Group B	58	92	10
Supervisor(s)	64	75	5 (eq)
02 Communication			
Self	94	75	5 (eq)
Co-worker Group A	42	99	3 (eq)
Co-worker Group B	71	100	1 (eq)
Supervisor(s)	75	75	5 (eq)
03 Problem-solving and Counselling			
Self	83	75	5 (eq)
Co-worker Group A	52	99	3 (eq)
Co-worker Group B	71	100	1 (eq)
Supervisor(s)	83	75	5 (eq)
04 Team Development			
Self	78	75	5 (eq)
Co-worker Group A	55	99	3 (eq)
Co-worker Group B	65	100	1 (eq)
Supervisor(s)	64	79	2 (eq)
05 Work Allocation			
Self	86	83	1 (eq)
Co-worker Group A	58	100	1 (eq)
Co-worker Group B	73	100	1 (eq)
Supervisor(s)	54	79	2 (eq)
06 Team Relationships			
Self	78	75	5 (eq)
Co-worker Group A	54	100	1 (eq)
Co-worker Group B	66	96	9
Supervisor(s)	67	75	5 (eq)
07 Delegation			
Self	72	75	5 (eq)
Co-worker Group A	48	94	11
Co-worker Group B	58	88	11
Supervisor(s)	72	75	5 (eq)
08 Quality Standards			
Self	79	79	3 (eq)
Co-worker Group A	46	99	3 (eq)
Co-worker Group B	64	98	5 (eq)
Supervisor(s)	83	75	5 (eq)
09 Objective Setting			
Self	89	75	5 (eq)
Co-worker Group A	48	99	3 (eq)
Co-worker Group B	62	98	5 (eq)
Supervisor(s)	47	85	1

As part of the workshop, he completed a self-rating on the 'Eleven Skills of Linking'. He wondered at the time, though, whether his team members might rate him the same or differently. He was fairly sure that his team was well balanced in terms of the Team Management Wheel, but recognised that balanced teams were some of the most difficult teams to link well. On returning to his work place, he decided to ask his team what they thought of him as a managerial linker.

At one of his regular team briefing sessions, he discussed the recent course he had taken and introduced the linking concept of the Team Management Wheel. He said that he would like everyone to complete the Linking Skills Index and that they would all discuss the results at the next meeting.

At that meeting, after discussing the team strengths and weaknesses, Richard then said he was interested in the team's discussing how well they thought the team was *linked*.

On two of the skills – *active listening* and *problem solving* – the team had given him a significantly lower score. Richard was surprised at this, but facilitated a lengthy discussion session trying to find out specifically where he was 'going wrong'. He learned a lot about their attitudes towards him, and was able to make some changes in his linking behaviour.

Richard's intervention technique was highly successful, partly because of his facilitation ability which he had learned earlier in his career as a management trainer. He was able to encourage positive criticism and receive it as advice on which he could act. People less skilled than Richard may have to use a consultant as a facilitator, otherwise the team members may be reluctant to 'open up' and indicate their true feelings.

Summary

The linker concept is a very important one in business today. Increasingly there are more and more professional people who are well educated and knowledgeable who can make or break a team.

The days when the manager could decide and tell other people what to do are gone. The manager today must be a problem-solver. Above all, managers are increasingly politicians within a network of people, not only in their own team, but between various parts of the organisation such as headquarters, divisions, suppliers, buyers, unions, government bodies and so on.

To be successful, team leaders need to have strong skills in linking. Our work suggests that today's manager needs to have not only technical skills of a high order, but interpersonal skills as well, particularly those of communication which are essential if the team is to be linked together into a high-performing unit. The successful executives of tomorrow will be those who have mastered the skills of managerial linking.

However, it is not just the managers who need to develop linking skills. All team members need to do so and improve their communication internally and externally.

How do you rate as a linker?

The direct way to find out is to complete a Linking Skills Index and ask your team and colleagues to do so. Then you will receive a report on their views which you can discuss. In this way you can develop ways to improve your performance.

7

TEAM MANAGEMENT SYSTEMS IN ACTION

Introduction

The concepts of Team Management described in the previous chapters can be used in a variety of ways to improve the quality of management in *all* organisations. We advocate a systematic approach to the application of the theories and have worked with many organisations to help them set up their own systems of management improvement. To date we have applied the techniques to situations ranging from recruitment to team-planning and problem-solving.

However, to know which instrument you should use it is important to follow the steps of:

1. Identify the business objectives (i.e. profit, quality, productivity levels).
2. Development strategies such as those listed on the continuum below.

Team Management

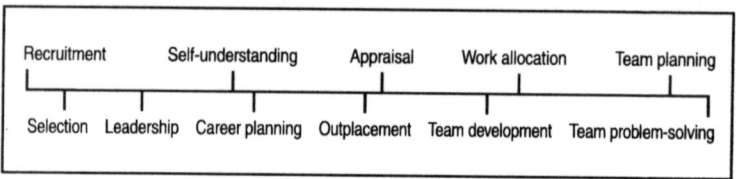

Figure 13. Team management systems applications.

3. Choice of feedback instruments to gain relevant data such as the TMI, TWI, TPI and LSI.

Some examples of these applications will help you see how high performance can be achieved in your organisation.

Recruitment and selection

Barrie Ffrench, former Director of Human Resources at Touche Ross Services Pty in Brisbane, Australia, has used the Team Management Index for recruitment. He has been selecting managers for many years and has used most of the 'personality test' instruments that are available. These instruments, he says, find out *something* about applicants but the question is, 'What is the precise accuracy of what is found out and, more importantly, what is its relevance to the job in question?' He likes the Team Management Index as it is work-based and he has had some outstanding successes in choosing the best applicants for executive positions. He reports:

'The selection process has four stages to it:

- proper definition of the assignment by talking out with the client what is actually needed in a new executive, and this can be done using the Types of Work Index to clarify the job requirements;
- designing the best advertising campaign or other method of attracting suitable clients;

[80]

- interviewing selected applicants and picking out those most likely to succeed; and
- discussing the short-listed applicants with nominated referees so that a probing analysis can be made of the strengths and weaknesses of each candidate.

'However, the TMI and TWI can assist in reducing the odds against failure. No selection process is certain, and it therefore follows that all recruitment is something of a gamble. Skilled and experienced recruiters are really in the business of reducing odds against failure: they look at as many factors as possible that influence success and failure, and apply these to each candidate. In effect, what they are doing is finding the person statistically most likely to succeed in the job (or, if you are a cautious person, the person least likely to fail).

'What the TMI and TWI do is give some valuable extra information on possibilities/probabilities. It is then up to us to make use of this information as part of a total picture. However, it is not the total picture itself.

'The TWI has been particularly useful in getting clients' specifications. This is most important because many heads of business find it difficult to articulate what their real requirements are. Experienced recruiters have found that the first time many executives can really identify what they are looking for is when they are confronted by two or three alternatives. They often choose instinctively, not in an orderly rational fashion. The TWI helps identify if the work preferences match the job demands.'

The creative accountant case

A major Australian engineering manufacturing company had created a new position for a cost accountant. It was very much a hands-on position; this person would work within the manufacturing environment, and would be responsible for keeping track of even the most minute costing detail associated with every project in an exceptionally busy environment. The job called for diligence and precision, and it did not allow much flexibility in the method of operation, but instead was a most reactive one, in the sense that the person appointed had to fit into the environment already existing.

The best applicant on paper was perfectly qualified both academically and in job experience. Following an interview, he still remained an extremely well-qualified applicant. However, the Team Management Index showed him to be a Creator-Innovator with very high scores for extroversion, creative information-gathering, and flexibility.

We discussed the TMI report by asking him first to read it, and then asked for his comments. On finishing the report, he looked up and said, 'This is me. Is this why I have been changing jobs so often?'

Despite the fact that he had been giving good service, he was becoming quickly bored with each job, and had not properly analysed the reasons for this boredom. He consequently disqualified himself from the application, and successfully went seeking a job more suited to the kind of role that he preferred to play. The organisation was also spared from making an appointment which appeared good on paper, but would, on all evidence available, have been a very short-lived one.

The loyal employee

A recruitment consultant was asked to find an executive for a manufacturing organisation, pretty much a family company and located in a provincial city. The applicant in question had a very similar background, and had recently left a family organisation engaged in heavy engineering manufacturing when it was taken over by a major multi-national organisation that proceeded to make the company simply an operating division of a fairly bureaucratic monolithic organisation. The TMI results showed the applicant to be an Upholder-Maintainer with a very high score for 'beliefs', with other role preferences being Concluder-Producer and Controller-Inspector.

The Upholder-Maintainer role became significant when we asked the applicant why he had left his last job when he was so highly thought of. His reply was significant: 'It just wasn't the same environment once Mr James no longer ran the company. I did not feel as if I belonged there.' Referee reports showed that if there was one characteristic more evident than the candidate's attention to detail in every form of financial reporting, it was his need to have intense loyalty to the organisation.

After 12 months, the report from his new employer was that he fitted the place 'like a glove'.

Sales representatives

Touche Ross have had the opportunity of observing a number of sales representatives and of comparing their success with their Team Management Roles. It is interesting to note that the more successful sales representatives ranged from Explorer-Promoter to Assessor-Developer, Thruster-Organiser and Concluder-Producer.

Different successful sales representatives go about their jobs in different ways. The Explorer-Promoter is often the better 'door-opener' – good at canvassing and acquiring new leads from new sources. He may also be the kind of sales representative who annoys head office because of an inattention to paperwork. Naturally, this need not occur because people's good sense can make them behave in a way that is not consistent with their natural inclinations.

Contrary to what might have been expected, we have noted a large number of very successful sales people in the Concluder-Producer role. Such people are good at getting orders and tying up details in the shortest possible time.

A personal experience is that the two-person sales team consisting of an Explorer-Promoter and a Concluder-Producer can be a very effective weapon. One sales person opens up sales opportunities; the other closes the sale in the shortest possible time.

Cloning

No matter how much we try not to, most of us tend to recruit people in our own image. Subconsciously, it appears that we imagine that those characteristics that we know we have are desirable ones for every job in the organisation. One organisation conducted a two-day top team performance programme as an exercise in team development. All had their preferred role in the Assessor-Developer sector. A 'Team Wheel' was put up on the wall, showing the 16 people all in the one role, and with related roles all clustered around it.

After a few moments' silence, and a couple of giggles, the Chief Executive asked: 'Could that be why nothing ever gets finished around here?'

Self-understanding

The Team Management Profiles and the Team Management Wheel can be used to set up a system for self-understanding in management teams. Self-understanding is particularly important for self-esteem and personal stability, as is highlighted by the case of Jack Butler.

Jack worked in a timber factory which produced a wide range of products based on pine trees. The raw materials for the factory were the vast pine forests which were scattered through the mountains surrounding the factory.

Jack was the Forest Manager, and on the Team Management Wheel he was an Upholder-Maintainer. He was a quiet person who really enjoyed his job. Much of his time was spent in the mountains supervising contract loggers. He enjoyed his trips through the forest and preferred the company of his dog to humans. Often he would plan a forest visit for a Friday so that he could spend his weekend in a log cabin he had built perched dose to a waterfall just below the snow line. Jack was an excellent fisherman and could do almost anything with his hands.

At work Jack was very well liked. Characteristically he was

very supportive of others even if on some occasions he was some-what self-effacing. At other times when his principles were infringed he became very forceful and had developed the knack of handling people who were aggressive.

The senior management of the company had decided that Jack had gone as far as he could in the organisation. This is a common conclusion people sometimes make about Upholder-Maintainers as they often don't push themselves forward at work as Thruster-Organisers usually do. In our analysis of TMIs only 2 per cent of them have been Upholder-Maintainers. However, they *are* there in the workplace and typically they are found as team members doing their job quietly and efficiently with no fuss.

The manager of the plant was a strong Thruster-Organiser and was particularly aggressive and hard-driving of his staff. It would be fair to say they disliked him and were happy to see him 'disappear' overnight when he took on the Divisional Manager and tried to 'roll' him.

The factory needed a replacement and while the Personnel Department considered the matter, Jack Butler was asked to take over as Acting Manager. Although the Divisional Manager considered that Jack lacked initiative he was impressed with his ability to smooth over difficulties and get the job done in a quiet way. During the next three months Jack performed the job excellently. He brought the team back together and soon got them working as one. As a result the Divisional Manager asked him to consider taking over the Manager's job on a permanent basis.

What the Divisional Manager didn't know was that Jack hated the role he was being pushed into. In terms of the Team Management Wheel, he was being forced to move over to the right-hand side operating in a position probably more suited to an Assessor-Developer, Thruster-Organiser or Concluder-Producer. Jack could *do* the job, as he showed during the three-month 'caretaker' period, but he found it quite stressful. After he completed a TMI and received a profile as one of the 'Upholder-Maintainers' his whole life changed. During one of our discussions with him he said:

[85]

Team Management

'For years I had thought there was something wrong with me. I prefer my own company but society and this organisation in particular prefers people who are more outgoing and 'pushy'. Actually I find these people very shallow and really I think they are missing out on important life experiences.

'I have high standards and believe everyone should be courteous and considerate of people's feelings. After all, people are our most important asset and should be given top priority even if it means taking decisions which are less than optimum in money terms.

'Throughout my life there have been pressures to make it as a senior manager. My mate Jim Davidson who started with me in the company 25 years ago considered everyone was a failure unless they made it to the top. He did, and last year he had a heart attack.

'So when I was offered the job of caretaker manager at first I was thrilled because I felt that at last I had been noticed. I have done the job to the best of my ability and they must have liked what I did or they wouldn't have asked me to stay on. What they don't know is every morning when I wake up I have butterflies in my stomach. I know that during the day I am going to have to deal with some unpleasant problem. I really get worked up when I have to deal with controversial issues and the stress has undoubtedly affected my home life. My wife said only this morning that I had become 'impossible to live with' since I've been Acting Manager.

'So when I read my Upholder-Maintainer profile it all clicked into place. People *are* different. We all have different strengths and should use them to advantage. There is nothing inferior about me. I bring to the organisation a wealth of experience in the job I do and it is done in a highly efficient way. I realise now that line management is not for me.'

Eventually Jack decided not to take on the job as factory manager and returned to his job as forest manager, knowing that it was 'OK' to be the way he was. When we recently spoke with him he had indeed taken a promotion but this time into the head office as Personnel Manager, a job he considered matched his preferences.

Leadership review

The Team Management technology also allows individuals to develop systems for improving their leadership effectiveness. We have already discussed Richard Peters, who used the eleven skills of linking to analyse how well he was leading his team. Now we shall talk about Don Jacobs, who used a rather novel intervention to get the team to talk about his leadership style.

It is unusual for senior managers to invite their team to review the performance of their leader. Normally the review process is the other way around – the leader reviews the team members. However, Don Jacobs decided to 'turn things upside down' and devise his own system for reviewing his leadership.

Don is a senior bank manager who participated in a public Team Management programme. He was impressed by the Team Management Wheel which helped him understand the strengths and weaknesses of both his own approach to management and also that of his team members. Upon receiving his Team Management Profile, he declared to the other programme members, 'I am going to photocopy this and send it to every member of my team.'

One of the participants asked why, and Don replied, 'I'm going to call a meeting and ask them whether they think this profile reflects the way I manage and what we can do as a team to make improvements.'

Another of the programme participants commented, 'Don't you think that's dangerous?'

Don Jacobs replied, 'I don't think so. If I set an example and show that I am willing to have people discuss my own approach to management, I believe it will encourage other people to be open and do the same.'

Don Jacobs went back to his team and did exactly as he said he would. He called a meeting and had everyone discuss the way the team was being led. Before doing so', he outlined the theory of the Team Management Wheel and asked the team where his approach fitted into the model. Next he gave them his Team Management Profile to read and this then led to a wide discussion on the strengths and weaknesses of the team and what they needed to do to improve.

All the team members were impressed with the accurate report on Don Jacobs, and asked whether they could have profiles done on themselves. Don arranged this and then convened a longer meeting to talk about the vision for the team and to plan for 'high performance'. Don was surprised at how open the team members were in talking about their profiles. Since that day, he believes his team has become more *energised*, and that their group meetings have been more productive.

Performance appraisal

Over the last twenty years management practices have become more professional, particularly in the area of objectives-setting and performance appraisal. The Types of Work Index and the Team Management Index and Wheel can be used to set up a powerful system for reviewing not only individual performance but also team performance.

Personal work reviews

Often these meetings go off track because the boss and the team member can have different views of the job. These can be clarified in advance by both completing the TWI. Then the job and the person's work preferences can be discussed in the context of the performance and changes made.

When running feedback sessions the Team Management Profile reports can therefore be used to provide a focus for the interview discussions. The manager and the team member can go through the report page by page and discuss the comments made under the various headings of 'work preferences' and job demands. Both parties can then relate the comments to the tasks that have been undertaken during the last year and the performance levels achieved. It also gives the manager and team member a chance to see how well the team member's preferences have been matched to the tasks that have been assigned. If the match is poor it may help explain under-achievement and also gives team members a chance to indicate the type of work they prefer and to request more overlap between task and preference in the future work to be allocated.

Team appraisal

Many organisations have what they call 'team appraisal' sessions but often these sessions are focused on 'content' and not the 'process'. We have attended several of these and usually found that they centre on meetings to assess whether a budget is on target or in variance. We have also seen, in engineering environments for example, meetings where the manager calls people together to assess whether the project is going according to the planned schedule. We have also been involved in many meetings where the manager calls people together on a regular weekly basis to hear reports from individuals. All of these can be called performance appraisal meetings. However, in themselves they are not sufficient. They deal mainly with the content and the task, and have very little to do with the process.

To make a real improvement in appraising effectiveness the team needs to concentrate on 'HOW things are done rather than on 'WHAT' is done. At meetings to discuss the 'HOW' it is vital to facilitate a discussion between people on what lies behind the facts and figures. This will usually mean a discussion on the behavioural aspects of the team.

Many managers don't encourage this because they are

concerned things may get out of hand, with people saying things they later regret. From our experience, however, if they are handled appropriately such meetings are positive and lead towards more effective teamwork.

In our work with aircrew team management we found that aircrews were very good on the hard facts and the details but weak when it came to the human processes. For example, we asked whether at the end of each flight they ever reviewed the flight just completed and discussed how things had gone. The answer was invariably 'no'. We therefore encouraged them to do so and showed them ways in which they could begin to share and compare data, and give each other feedback. As a result many of them tried a review session and found it very helpful. In particular the younger pilots began to learn a lot more and there was an increasing *esprit de corps* amongst all pilots.

The same principles apply in factories and offices. It is vital that the manager has an opportunity to get together with team members and talk over how they are working with each other. The feedback should be two-way between the manager and the team and also laterally with team members giving feedback to one another.

The rules of the game are to ensure that feedback is positive rather than negative. A brief description of the offending behaviour can be made, but then the discussion should concentrate on what to do so that things are improved next time. Feedback then becomes 'constructive' rather than 'destructive'. The aim should be to turn sessions of 'criticism' into sessions of 'giving advice'.

When managers do this they are acting in the 'linker' role by facilitating the interaction of the views and feelings of team members. The focus should be on improving performance and becoming a high-performing team. Therefore all comments and discussion should be directed to this end.

Our Team Performance Index has had a powerful effect on team appraisal. The data the team receives is comparative and from people who count. Discussing how to respond and take action to improve provides the focus a team needs to improve.

Career planning

The Team Management Profiles and Wheel can form the basis of a systematic approach to career planning. Today, responsibility for career planning should rest mainly with the individual. If you wait for an organisation to plan your career for you and to choose the various placements which extend you, then you may be bitterly disappointed. Unless you firmly grasp hold of your career and plan your own career journeys, then your full potential may be unrealised.

Very often in career planning workshops we will ask participants to review their career journeys in terms of the Team Management Wheel. Where were they five years ago, ten years ago, twenty years ago? Where will they be in five years' time, ten years' time?

To do this successfully it is necessary to understand how the various constructs map on to the Team Management Wheel. This is dealt with in Chapter 8.

The line manager

One common career journey we have noticed with line managers is the 'anti-clockwise' drift from Concluder-Producer to Assessor-Developer, as shown in Figure 14. Many young professionals – particularly engineers and accountants – start work with preferences for introversion, practical information-gathering, analytical decision-making and structured organisation (IPAS). This maps them firmly into the Concluder-Producer sector of the Wheel. Often they work here very effectively for several years, concentrating on their technical work and supervising small teams.

Over a period of years their introversion preference at work will often move towards the extroversion side of the relationships construct as they learn through experience and management development programmes to become more outgoing. This starts them on a journey into the Thruster-Organiser sector (EPAS) (extroverted, practical, analytical and structured) where they are often very effective as project managers, making things happen on time and to budget.

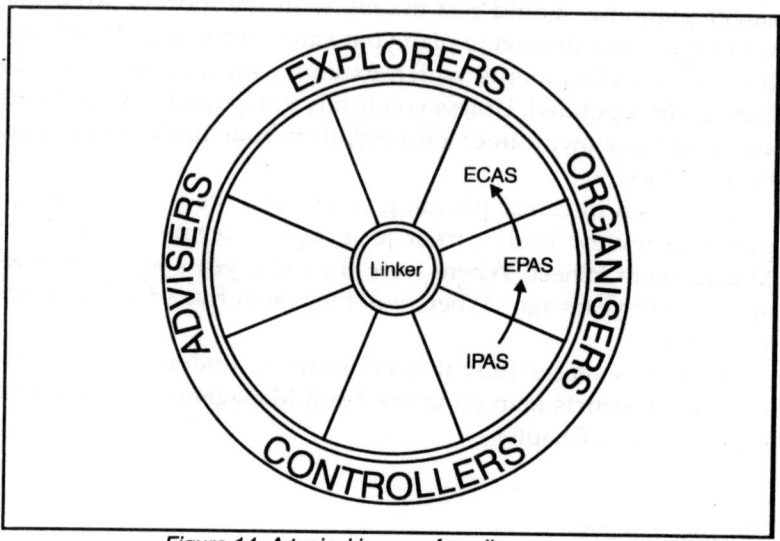

Figure 14. A typical journey for a line manager.

Many people may stay in this sector for several years but some continue their journey onwards. Again through management development, mentoring, coaching, experience, or even their own desire, many managers move their preference on the information-gathering construct. They are encouraged to take a more 'helicopter' view of the workplace and look towards 'what might be' rather than 'what is'. This causes them to move from the practical side of the construct towards the creative side. As a result they move further anti-clockwise on the Wheel into the Assessor-Developer sector, nicely poised between the 'Exploring' and 'Organising' parts of the Wheel.

TEAM MANAGEMENT SYSTEMS IN ACTION

The research and development scientist

Many people who start off their careers in research and development have a preference for the Creator-Innovator sector of the Team Management Wheel. Often they are introverted, creative, analytical and flexible (ICAF) in terms of the constructs, and many of them have a higher degree (Masters or Doctorate). Whether their work preferences caused them to follow this career or whether their preferences were moulded *by* their career is an interesting subject for debate. Organisations like Hewlett-Packard often have many of their R & D people with this pattern of scoring.

These R & D scientists often work for many years on their own or in small groups developing new products, processes or services for the organisation. We have noticed their development going in one of two ways as indicated in Figure 15.

As the scientists are pushed into managerial roles, supervising the work of a project team, the culture of the organisation often forces them to become more structured. There are monthly reports to produce, budgets to draw up and report on, meetings to prepare for and so on. This often causes a journey to take place from the flexible end of the *organisation* construct towards the structured end. For many this is not an easy transition and to be effective a lot of support needs to be given to the person undergoing the transition.

The net effect of this change is to move the person from the Creator-Innovator sector to the Thruster-Organiser sector. Often people with this pattern of TMI scoring will have a split Wheel, straddling both the Creator-Innovator and Thruster-Organiser sectors. They enjoy working with and developing ideas but then have to move to the other side of the Wheel and 'thrust' and 'organise' them so that action takes place. Once this is done they may well want to retreat back into the comfort zone of their Creator-Innovator sector.

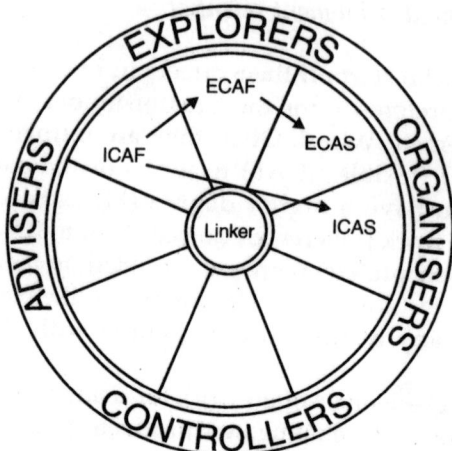

Figure 15. A typical career journey for a research and development scientist.

Instead of moving directly across to the 'organising' sector of the Wheel some ICAF scientists go on a clockwise drift around the Wheel. As they are promoted into managerial roles they soon learn that they have to become more outgoing if they are to successfully interact with their team. As a result they become more extroverted and move towards the Explorer-Promoter sector (ECAF), persuading and influencing other managers in the organisation to take up their ideas and commercialise them.

Many stay in this sector for several years, but some may continue their journey around to the Assessor-Developer sector as they learn to become more structured in the way they work, adhering to the company culture, which for middle and senior managers is often 'AS' – analytical and structured.

These two examples highlight the type of career journeys that managers do undertake. Nobody remains in the one sector all their managerial life. People grow and change jobs and as they do their map on the Team Management Wheel will change. However, the change is a slow function of time and the career journeys usually take a number of years.

Where are you now on the Wheel? Where are you aiming for? What might you need to do to get there?

Outplacement

In these days when people move on voluntarily, or have to be reassigned duties due to changes in business direction, it is important to have a tool which will help people make the right choice for the future.

The Team Management Index has been used on many occasions to help with both promotion and outplacement decisions. On each occasion, the individual has been asked to complete the Team Management Index and this is used as the basis of a counselling session.

Bob Baker was a case in point. Due to the closure of the business in which he was working, he asked for outplacement advice. As part of the counselling session, he discussed his profile with an outplacement consultant. He said, 'I found the information I received most useful, as I had not clearly identified where my interests and strengths were. It enabled me to look more specifically for the kind of jobs that I should apply for.'

When he went for interviews, he took a copy of his Team Management Profile with him and gave it to his prospective employer. He found this approach very useful as an 'icebreaker' to direct the interview in a way that was most useful for him. This enabled him to quickly ascertain whether 'what they wanted' was 'what he wanted'. It wasn't long before Bob found a job as Administration Manager, something he considered matched his preference as a Controller-Inspector.

Work allocation

Jack Young was a person who was enthused about developing his team, but was not sure how to go about it. He knew that he had a lot of intelligent and motivated people in his group, but they didn't seem to work too well together.

He therefore consulted us on how to improve the effectiveness of his team. As a result, a one-day team development workshop was held where the Team Management Wheel was presented, and the team members had a chance to read their team profiles.

During the meeting it was suggested that it might be helpful if everyone shared their profiles and read the comments about each other. This led to a very interesting and open discussion about people's strengths and weaknesses.

Following this, Young asked the team how they felt they should develop in order to tackle the tasks before them. It was generally agreed that there was a need for greater cooperation.

Young discussed with the team how this could be achieved. Several people indicated that perhaps they should consider re-allocating some of the work so that it matched people's preferences more closely. A discussion ensued and a number of specific ideas were put forward as possible ways of improving teamwork. Sub-groups of the team were formed and they agreed to go away and come up with definite proposals at the next meeting.

At this meeting, the team reported that considerable progress had been made and that there had been some rearrangement of duties so that people's strengths were used more effectively. In particular, some *exploring* work currently done by a Concluder-Producer had been exchanged for more detailed work currently done by an Explorer-Promoter. Both parties said they were very pleased with the changes and felt 'rejuvenated'. The team said that their various meetings had been tremendous and that the team was now using everyone's skills more effectively and in a complementary way.

Team development

Many organisations have used the Team Management Instruments and Wheel to improve the working of teams. In doing so they have usually devised their own development systems to suit the culture of the organisation. In all cases the Team Management reports and the Team Management Wheel are used to get team members to think about their strengths and weaknesses.

Hong Kong Bank

Ray Campsie and Mike Harpham of the Hong Kong Bank Teamwork Development Unit (TWD) are typical of the users of Team Management Systems. By September 1987 they had gained credibility amongst a small group of middle managers and were looking for a 'tool' to capture the imagination and commitment of a very senior management team who regarded themselves as highly experienced managers. They report their experiences as follows:

The Team Management Index helped us break through the resistance of senior managers to talk about interpersonal problems. In particular the set of techniques generally known as Team Management Systems–

(a)   prompted very positive feedback to and for the TWD unit;

(b)   encouraged an atmosphere whereby it was legitimate to talk about feelings in senior management teams as well as thinking;

(c)   focused busy managers on the essential links between task and process (and provided clues on how to manage that boundary);

(d)   provided personal style feedback and team implications for these very senior staff;

(e)   opened up communication channels between levels of management.

The Team Management Index undoubtedly gained high credibility with all those who used it. It is swift to administer, easy to

[97]

explain, detailed in output, and provides a powerful and easily understood visual snapshot of team strengths and weaknesses.

Management trainers are creative types and it was not long before the TWD Unit took up the baton and moulded the original model to specific use. A workbook was developed which guided participants through the implications of the data for themselves and their teams. Success bred more development and a 'kit' was introduced which enabled managers to cascade Teamwork Development through their business divisions in a systematic way.

The power of the Wheel has resulted in an expansion of its use beyond the most senior teams and it now provides the core of a two-week in-house senior management programme in which a team is developed and then involved in an action-learning business project. This programme has now become our main source of new clients below top team level. We have used Team Management Systems in many countries – Hong Kong, Malaysia, Philippines, Singapore, India, Australia, the Middle East, Japan, USA – and it has been enthusiastically received by all who have sought to use its power to bring teams together through the sharing of a common mode of teamwork.

How do we use TMS to move a group of individuals into a high-performing (or at least higher performing) team?

After the group has decided on criteria of team effectiveness, we use the Team Management Profiles to start a process of 'opening up' which often ends with a very intensive session where all members give and receive feedback. We achieve the 'opening up' by letting each member reflect on their profile alone, and then share the implications with a colleague; sometimes we hand out opposite profiles to help in this exercise. By this time members have a good understanding of the Team Management Wheel, finding it easy to discuss even the most personal issues, and they then put the individual roles together to form a Team Wheel. The level of energy, already high, never fails to rise when the group discusses the team implications of *their* Team Wheel. As a result the commitment to planning action is great.

After this session, the group has moved from 'being a group' towards starting its development into a team. Most teams put their Wheel to one side and then move into an action planning mode which encompasses both intra-team and inter-team issues.

TMS has allowed our TWD Unit to gain great credibility and to move faster than would otherwise have been possible into key process areas – a point.made clear when we clarify that because of time commitments only two (very full) days are available for our work. So thank you TMS and of course, its creators!

Hewlett-Packard

In Europe, Hewlett-Packard, the very first corporate users of TMS, has developed similar systems to help sales divisions and customer-support divisions improve their effectiveness. Jacques Dufrenne, one of the first TMS accredited trainers, introduced the Team Management Wheel to customer support managers. He reports:

There was a need to improve teamwork between the various department managers so that customer satisfaction improved when problems occurred. This was our first use of TMS which has now been used with over 1600 managers throughout Europe.

Most of our intervention work has been targeted to specific individual problems in teams. Many teams have potential conflict problems and TMS has been very successful here as it shows participants why they are having problems and what to do to solve them.

After months or even years, previous participants have called us requesting follow-up sessions or asking for another programme since the team composition had changed.

[99]

Team Management

Many participants mention the high return on investment the High-Performing Teams programme has achieved. In general the programme has immediate visible and measurable results on the business they are working in. Examples are:

- projects go much faster than before
- sales force effectiveness grows
- marketing plans are implemented in a smoother way
- effectiveness in complex organisations is higher
- the tasks are allocated to match team roles and therefore performance is enhanced
- morale in groups is higher and so is the productivity.

The flexibility of the course is a real advantage as the subjects covered permit extension to other issues such as

- advanced leadership
- creative teamwork
- human interaction
- decision-making
- interviewing.

Team-planning

By choosing when to use the TMI, the LSI and the TPI you can make a big impact on teams by giving them the data to take action.

Following on from any team development session it is often useful to run a team-planning session where the team considers 'where is it going?' and 'how will it get there?' A three-stage system for doing this involves:

- Agreeing the team's mission, vision and values
- Conducting a strategic performance analysis
- Setting objectives.

Mission, vision and values

Most organisations today have a corporate 'mission' – simply what the organisation 'stands for' and what it is trying to achieve. Teams also need a 'mission' and it is important, particularly with new teams, to run a meeting where this is openly discussed. Unless people have a common understanding of what individuals want to achieve, then it is likely that everyone will be pulling in different directions.

Associated with the 'mission' is a clear statement of the 'values' that are important to each team member. Values are the underlying beliefs inherent in all of us that will motivate us to do our best. Values lead to the establishment of a team identity and team culture. Again, unless these are openly discussed then the team is unlikely to act as a coherent unit.

In establishing the mission of the team it is also necessary to have a clear 'vision' of where the team is heading in the next one, three and five years. What will it be like to work in this team in one, three, or five years' time? What will you see, feel and hear? What is the vision of excellence that each member has?

Our experience suggests that the mission/vision/values meeting should be specially convened and separated from any other team issues that need to be discussed. The meeting will probably take at least half a day, but it will enable team members to understand and discuss their role and function in the total organisation. On the surface it may appear to be obvious, but unless time is allocated to discussing the issues then problems can arise. Indeed in our experience the psychological effect of bringing people together to discuss the overall mission and purpose of the team can be a powerful welding and motivating device in itself.

Strategic performance analysis

A strategic analysis of the team's strengths, weaknesses, opportunities and threats is an essential planning tool that should be done at least once a year. This is the familiar SWOT analysis, originally established as a corporate planning tool but now often used at all levels in the organisation.

Strengths analysis
Here the team should discuss what they consider are the key strengths of the team and what might be done to reinforce and build on the strengths. Very often individuals and teams take their strengths for granted and do not subject them to a proper discussion. As a result the team does not develop or build on what is a major source of its success. Time should therefore be set aside for a thorough examination of what the team does well and how it can be further improved.

Weakness analysis
It is important that a team examines the areas where it does not do too well. These sessions can become destructive if not facilitated well, but if handled with care and understanding they can be the basis for major improvements. If a team can't criticise itself in an open and non-threatening way then it is unlikely to improve.

Opportunities analysis
The team needs to identify what the opportunities are for it to perform well during the next year. The best innovations or successes often come from meetings to discuss what opportunities there are to be grasped. These opportunities will often lead to a marketing 'niche' which can be successfully exploited.

Threats analysis
An identification of threats is essential if a team is to become 'high-performing'. These threats maybe internal or external and may be 'content' based or 'process' based. Once they are identified then plans can be drawn up to take account of each scenario and the team will then have a system to deal with each eventuality. Just thinking through and talking about

potential threats to the team will often thwart the inhibiting factors of anxiety and apprehension.

Objectives

The objectives of a team relate very much to the tasks they have to perform over a short time frame – perhaps the next six months. Objectives should always be framed in a specific output-oriented way. To achieve this it is necessary to discuss

- what has to be done
- when it has to be done
- who is to do it
- how it is to be done.

In many situations the first objective may need to be given to the team by the leader, particularly if the team is working closely with other teams on a large task. For example, in the production of cars, it is no use one department setting an objective which does not relate to what other departments are doing. However, once a team knows what the objective is, it is important that they are involved in the discussion of the other three questions. That is, team members should be able to make a contribution on who should do each task, how the task should be done and when it should be scheduled. Managers need to set up appropriate systems so these issues can be dealt with clearly.

Team problem-solving

Team Management Systems can be used to help a team solve difficult problems. There is potential synergy in a team particularly if it is a multi-preference one where multiple descriptions will be forthcoming.

One particular manager who worked with us had a team who

were primarily Organisers and Controllers. They worked in a factory environment and were very practical and well organised. However, as the manager said, 'We never seem to come up with new ways of doing things.'

This particular factory was responsible for producing cardboard boxes and there was a major problem facing them in competition. To survive they would have to cut their costs by 10 per cent or else risk 'going under'. The factory was run in a highly effective and efficient manner and the standard costing system was already adhered to by all staff. The manager recognised that there was probably potential to reduce costs further but that it would require a particularly 'creative' effort by all the team.

To 'balance' the team he hired one of us as a consultant and a systematic cost reduction improvement plan was developed which followed a practical, structured approach to the generation of creative solutions.

An initial meeting was held with the team and it was explained that over the next several weeks a number of half-day workshops would be held where any ideas for cost reduction would be discussed. Each person was asked to consider which area of the plant would be most suitable for cost reduction and to come up with their best idea of how to do it. Out of fifteen people there were twenty ideas generated.

The team met several times over the next few months and each idea was systematically examined. If the team agreed that the idea had merit then a task force was set up to investigate the idea. Each task force was 'balanced' as well as possible from amongst the various team members.

Within three months, over a quarter of a million dollars had been saved and the team was beginning to make real improvements, not only in the financial side but in the way they worked together. Note that the team had not changed; the direction of work emphasis in the meetings was carefully moved towards the north of the Wheel, but in a way that was acceptable to the hard-nosed' practical production people. Previous creative ideas had been ignored because the group was composed of people who had a low preference for this type of activity.

Problem-solving meetings such as the one described work best if they are held away from the place of work. They should be held for at least one day, or more if the team can manage to be away from work for a longer period. The meetings should be focused on 'creativity' and any inputs should be logged for discussion and not immediately shot down by others. Judgements should be suspended until people have had an opportunity to consider the suggestions.

Whenever an idea is put forward, people should seek the facts to support it, rather than having it knocked down on the basis of opinion. It is in this environment that you will find people start to put forward good ideas as well as weak ones. So long as the atmosphere is supportive then ideas which can be implemented will be forthcoming.

This systematic technique for problem-solving can be applied to any major problem a team is facing – be it costs, productivity, safety, throughput, efficiency or some other issue.

8

ACTION PLANS FOR TEAM
DEVELOPMENT

Introduction

In the last chapter we described the Team Management Systems that can be used to develop your team. In this chapter we highlight the need for action plans, all involving team 'interventions' which can be applied during the course of your daily interactions with the team. Please try out some of them, and develop your own systems to apply the ideas.

What you need to do is develop a planned approach to improving team performance. Changes do not happen quickly and it will certainly take time to move your team from a low-performing one into a high-performing unit. Many groups we have worked with have a year-long programme of team events all designed to improve team performance. At the end of the year the results are increased productivity, higher levels of commitment and output, improved cooperation, better communication, more ideas and creativity, and generally a higher level of 'energy'.

Winning teams

Everyone likes to be on a winning side.

It is important therefore to create an atmosphere where members of your team see that they can win both individually and collectively. The way you manage people in your team will determine whether they are winners or losers. To start with they have got to get a firm commitment in their heads that they can win.

One of our clients – a factory manager – recently took us round his factory. He introduced us to people on the shop floor and it was clear that he had an excellent rapport with the operators. As he introduced us we noticed that he was also gathering data on the way work was progressing and was noting down points that were raised with him by the operators. When we got back to his office he said: 'The people out there are the people who make this place tick. They're real champions, every one of them.'

His very language, talking of champions, signalled his attitude to his people and the job. As he said, 'Every day we have to get material produced and distributed in order to serve our customers. We can only do that if people believe that they are on a winning team.'

Therefore he set the pace by letting people know what was required and then regularly informing them whether they were achieving targets. He would wander round the factory talking not only to the supervisors, but to people on the shop floor as well, using such phrases as 'we're winning' or 'we're doing well'. Throughout, his message was a positive one, reinforcing success wherever he saw it and encouraging extra performance where he saw problems.

Do your team members see themselves as a group of winners? If not, what can you do about it? Perhaps the first thing is to call members of the group together and ask them what winning means to them. Ask them what the team does well and what it does badly. Then invite them to develop plans to improve in all the areas mentioned.

[107]

Initially it may not be easy. There may be all sorts of external problems over which the team feels it has little control. The important thing is to identify these problems and then start to develop ways and means by which they can be solved. There should be a team effort, with all members contributing rather than everything being left to you as an individual. The manager's job is to conduct the orchestra, not try to play all the instruments.

When you see positive results, let people know. Indeed, share both the failures and successes. Once the team can see what is happening, they can begin to make changes to improve their performance. Above all, your job as the manager is to give your team permission to win. Let them know it is important to you. Let them know that they can succeed, and involve them wherever possible in the process of leading a winning team.

Meetings

All managers have meetings with their team. These can be formal or informal meetings.

Formal meetings

Meetings can be classified in terms of the Team Management Wheel into Exploring meetings or Organising meetings. Exploring meetings are held to share information and look at 'where are we going?' Often decisions are not forthcoming but everyone's views and ideas are exchanged.

Organising meetings are the ones where definite decisions are made and actions assigned. Objectives are set and everyone has a clear idea of what is expected of them.

What are your meetings like? Do you have too many Organising meetings and not enough Exploring meetings? Or is it the other way round? Review your meetings over the last twelve months and see what sort of a balance you have.

Agendas

To gain commitment to the meeting, it is important that people have an opportunity to put forward what they regard as important. Therefore at least seven to ten days in advance of a business meeting people should be invited to put forward their agenda items.

This is normal practice and in most organisations forms the basis upon which teams can begin to resolve issues. However, on the day of a meeting there may be other important issues which have arisen. Therefore prior to starting a meeting, always ask members if they have any additional matters they want to raise.

Remember the 'two-thirds' rule when drawing up the agenda. At least two-thirds of the topics should involve *everyone* invited to the meeting. If this is not the case then you may well have two meetings disguised as one.

Look at the agenda of your last few meetings, and question how useful the items are. Consider also your process for getting those items on to the agenda. Who for example decides them? How could you go about setting an agenda which reflects the concerns of all of those people who will be attending?

Team-briefing meetings

Team-briefings have become very popular over the last few years. They tend to be semi-formal meetings focused more towards Exploring and Advising than to Controlling and Organising.

Managers and supervisors are responsible for passing information to their team and the whole process cascades down from the top. However, the meeting should not be a 'one-way' affair and equal emphasis needs to be given to encouraging team members to talk about their problems. In that way information can flow back, upwards through the organisation.

Team-briefing meetings are essential if the team is to be well linked. In fact the concept of team-briefing is one of the key skills of Linking.

[109]

Team Management

Informal meetings

We have heard a lot about MBWA (management by walking around) and also the 'one-minute manager'. The main message from these approaches is that managers should try to keep in touch with the detail but without interfering. This is a skill which needs to be learned and practised.

Essentially as a manager you need to keep in touch with sufficient detail to know what is going on. Once you have found out, you can then make arrangements for the matter to be dealt with. The great advantage of regular casual informal contact with people is that they learn how to communicate the key points of importance to you.

It is the people at the 'coal face' who know what is happening minute by minute, day by day. In reality there are no one-minute quick fixes. However, there are 'one-minute' opportunities where you can show your interest, enthusiasm and commitment to all the workers in your organisation. It is this approach that is the key to success for many managers.

Outputs

All teams have to produce results. However, individual members of teams often do not seem to know what the overall team is trying to do. Consequently we frequently find team members either not pulling in the same direction or not giving their best effort.

It is important, therefore, to sit down with the team and discuss what the outputs are. Too often teams start by working on the inputs. They will tell you what jobs have to be done, how many hours have to be allocated, how much money has to be spent, what the problem issues are and so on. All of these are concerned with inputs.

Therefore the whole team needs to meet together to focus on outputs and look at the forces which are likely to get in the way.

Once these forces are listed, an action plan to combat them can be developed.

Challenging targets

All teams need to have targets which are sufficiently stretching to make the work interesting, but not so difficult that the result is an attitude of despair amongst the team. The successful manager will know exactly what the balance is between making tasks too difficult or too easy.

People develop when they have to stretch themselves; so it is with a team. Therefore consider the challenges you are posing to the team. Are they having an easy ride, jumping the same fences as yesterday – or can you give them new hurdles to 'fly over'? Many people will say they dislike tasks which are too easy rather than those which are too hard. If they have a choice they will often opt for the one which is more difficult because it produces more 'challenge'.

Consider reviewing the challenges you set the team on a regular basis. Get the team together and discuss:

- How well do you feel we are doing?
- Are we shooting at the right targets'?
- What do we need to do to keep ahead?

It is simple questions like these that start a really good debate – providing you are prepared to give people the permission to be constructively critical. Therefore be systematic about improvement – encourage people on a regular basis to consider with you the new challenges they can set to improve not only themselves but also the business organisation.

Charting results

It is important for a team to see how it is performing. Sporting teams can quickly get feedback: they can tell whether they are winning or losing by counting the score. A work team needs to be able to do the same.

Therefore identify the measures by which the team can see how it is performing. Some of these will be straightforward, such as costs against budget. Others may be more difficult to work out, such as overall productivity. Equally, not all teams will have the revenue function against which to chart their income. However, all teams can measure their performance in terms of achieving particular objectives within a specific time and cost.

What are the critical success factors in your team? Agree with your team how these should be measured and then arrange to 'chart' them for all to see. The feedback from the TMS Instruments provides the data for individuals and teams to assess how others perceive their work.

Team communication

Most teams we have worked with indicate that communication could be improved. It seems almost to be a universal problem. Why is this? Clearly it is difficult to keep everyone in the picture all the time when there are so many things going on – new products, new technology, new markets, new ideas, new people and a host of other changes as well.

However, from our experience we find that teams don't always communicate well. For example, they put other matters higher on the order of priority. They are often too busy doing the work to communicate to others what it is all about. People don't attend meetings, or they fail to write reports, or often don't read the relevant documents. All these are regular issues which teams have to confront.

The linking task of the manager is to coordinate all the

'players' on the team and to make sure that each member knows what the others are doing. This requires some discipline and the planning of regular meetings. It means putting meeting dates into diaries as much as twelve months ahead and keeping to those dates. It means convincing people that these meetings are important and that everyone must attend.

Excellence in communication means developing the flexibility to interact with people in different ways. Different approaches need to be used with Explorer-Promoters as against Controller-Inspectors. One set of strategies may work with Thruster-Organisers but fail with Reporter-Advisers.

Both of us have written extensively on communication and we refer you to our books on the subject (McCann, 1988; Margerison, 1990).

One of the best ways to develop communication skills in your team is to encourage individuals or sub-groups in the team to give small presentations at meetings. These may be only half an hour long, but they enable everyone to get up and show what they are doing and what they have achieved. This not only helps communication but motivation as well. Therefore organise as many presentations as you can on as many topics as possible so that people become well informed. In the process of doing this you will be developing your team members as excellent communicators.

Seeing what they say

A very important aspect of team work is to help people solve problems and come to decisions quickly. Too much time is wasted in teams when people talk about the job rather than doing it. Sometimes teams become so bogged down in discussions that very little is ever resolved.

Decision-making in teams can often be enhanced if you help your group learn how to visualise what they say. This can be done by using visual aids such as whiteboards and flip charts. Help your team members to record their ideas in visual format so that everyone can see what they are thinking. If you rely on verbal format only you are ignoring one of our most important senses. Sight and sound will allow a double description of problems rather than the single description provided by either sense alone.

Some people are quite shy about writing on boards unless they have got their thoughts well ordered. It is important therefore to train people in putting forward half-formed views so that other people can comment and develop them. The problem here is that if the right atmosphere does not exist then people may criticise and judge everything that is put down. People should be trained to suspend judgement until they have got the facts and the ideas.

Problem-solving is a creative process and the more people can express themselves by visualising what they are saying the more likely it is that the team will begin to function effectively. You will get more done in a shorter time and the talk will become more meaningful. Agreements will be developed as a function of people visualising what they are talking about.

Some people will find it easier to visualise their thinking than others. On the Team Management Wheel these are the people who map into the Creator-Innovator and Explorer-Promoter sectors – the 'internal visual' people (McCann, 1988). These people often think in pictures and are more effective contributors to problem-solving when the whole process is conducted visually, as on whiteboards. Other sectors of the Team Management Wheel (Thruster-Organiser and Concluder-Producer) have stronger 'auditory channels' and are often more effective during the verbal phases. As your team will probably have a mixture of people from all round the Wheel, it pays to use both the visual and verbal formats in all your team discussions.

Summary

Teamwork is only a means to the end of improving performance. Such performance will be manifested in outputs like:

- increased sales
- reduced costs
- improved productivity
- better safety records
- higher quality products
- more new products.

This is the hard evidence of effective teamwork. Alongside this we would expect to find in teams that achieve the above more subjective indicators, such as:

- increased job satisfaction
- lower absenteeism
- more effective staff development
- increased cooperation
- a high *esprit de corps*
- high levels of motivation.

This chapter has outlined various techniques, methods, ideas, systems and procedures and processes you can consider. There is no one particular method which will solve all problems. However, the energy of your team can be substantially raised if you put into practice the action plans suggested here. In doing so you will be acting as a 'linker' – coordinating the team into a high-performing unit. Remember your job is to conduct the orchestra, not play all the instruments. The essence of effective teamwork is top team management. You can be a top team manager if you take on the key role as a linker, remember that outputs are important, and concentrate on the team processes.

9

RESEARCH DATA

Introduction

The personal Team Management Index (TMI) is a central focus of the Team Management Systems we have developed. It is the TMI that enables managers to gain an insight into the relationship between an individual's work preference and the team roles that need to be undertaken if a team is to be high-performing. The TMI allows managers to map their team on to the Team Management Wheel. As a result managers can then begin to:

- understand their own work preferences
- see how these fit into the team roles that are required
- discuss their preferences and roles with others in the team
- make adjustments for themselves and the team in order to improve performance.

Any instrument like the personal Team Management Index needs to be reliable and valid. In this chapter we summarise some of the more important psychometric studies which show the substance and validity of our 'teamwork technology tools'.

In order to set the work on the Team Management Index and Team Management Wheel in its proper context we will first look at the sociological and psychological aspects of teamwork. It is from these roots that our work has evolved. We have, however, introduced significant new dimensions to previous work and developed a powerful set of tools for managers to understand and develop more effective teamwork.

Sociological aspects of team management

When people work together they do so not just as individuals but in roles which fit the demands of the organisation. It is by the formation and taking of roles (as Weber, 1946, 1947, noted) that bureaucracies are established. People relate to each other not only in terms of their own personality and interests but in terms of role definitions and the expectations of others.

In his book *Explorations in Management*, the late Lord Wilfred Brown (1960) outlined the ways in which work roles could form the basis of modern organisation. This followed on from other similar industrial analyses such as those conducted by Chester Barnard (1938) in his book *The Functions of the Executive*. These approaches provide clear examples from experience in industry of how the sociology of teamwork was the very foundation of the modern organisation.

Role functions in organisations are quite distinct at, say, the Board level where there are usually key role distinctions between the Finance Director, the Production Director, the Personnel Director, the Marketing Director and, of course, the Managing Director. Similar functional role definitions occur at all levels of the organisation, even down to the individual members of the team, although in this case they may not always be easily recognised.

However, in addition to the functional roles there is also a team

[117]

role that describes how an individual contributes to the work of the team. An accountant, for example, has a finance functional role but the way this role is executed in the team can vary greatly.

Belbin (1981) went some way towards clarifying team roles in his book *Management Teams*. Here he identified different kinds of roles in management teams – roles such as *shapers, company workers, resource investigators,* etc. These roles were an attempt to describe the sociology of the team and explain how people took on a *behavioural* role depending on their own interests and the requirements of the situation.

In our work we have taken this sociological approach further and shown that people have particular *work preferences* that relate to the roles they play in a team. A knowledge of these roles and their relationship to individual work preferences is essential if the team is to become a *high-performing* one.

Psychological aspects of team management

Much work has been done on the psychology of small groups and their behaviour. The group dynamics movement has put forward numerous studies and interpretations of how individuals contribute to the effectiveness of groups. This psychological approach has emphasised everything from individual preferences and personality through to the way in which individuals interact with each other in both social and task-oriented groups. Zander (1982) has discussed many of these in his book *Making Groups Effective*.

The work of Bales (1950), Deutsch (1949), Janis (1972), and Shaw (1981), as well as Cartwright and Zander (1968) and Weick (1979), has shown how individuals can be affected by group processes. Others such as Likert (1976) have been more concerned with showing the impact of individual style and strategies on group performance. Still others, such as Eysenck (1977), have emphasised personality factors such as extroversion and introversion and the way they influence behaviour in groups.

[118]

However, it has been the work of Carl Jung (1923) in his book *Psychological Types* that has opened up considerable debate on the way individual preferences influence behaviour, and in particular how these preferences are manifested when people interact. It is this perspective which has influenced greatly our work on team management.

While we accept that group behaviour is a function of the task, the roles that people play, and the norms and values operating, i.e. *sociological aspects,* we also believe that the individual preferences and skills that people bring to a team are key *psychological factors* influencing individual and team performance. The combination of these factors has resulted in our managerial approach to understanding teams.

A management focus

The management approach to teamwork involves understanding individual preferences and developing ways of predicting how individual behaviour will impact on the outputs of the team. The sociological approach involves understanding the roles that are necessary in the team to ensure that the work is delivered and then managing the team according to the assigned roles. The management approach combines these two by assigning roles in the team according to the tasks and individual preferences and then linking the roles together into a coherent whole. It is this approach which has enabled us to develop the Team Management Wheel as a valuable tool for team development.

Figure 16 summarises the different approaches. The Myers-Briggs Type Indicator is an example of the psychological approach, whereas the Belbin theories have resulted from the sociological approach. The Margerison-McCann Team Management Wheel is the result of original research that identifies the link between team tasks and personal work preferences.

[119]

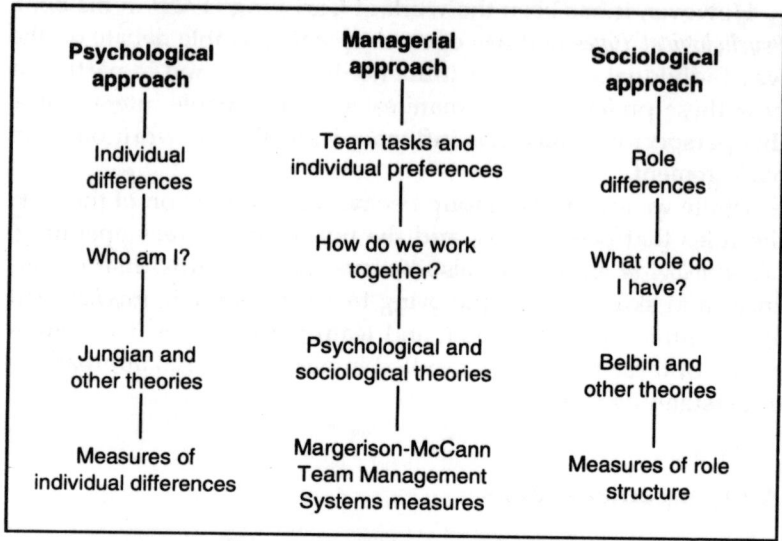

Figure 16. Different approaches to understanding people.

The need for a work preference measure

Previous work in the field has described the need for individual preferences and team roles to complement each other, but has not produced an accurate measure which managers can use on a day-to-day basis. Our work has now achieved this through the mapping process of the Team Management Wheel.

The method of measurement we chose was the self-declared work preferences of managers and their team members. The Team Management Index was created specifically for this purpose and went through over 20 iterations to reach its present form. The research described here was an integral part of that iterative process of improvement, based on scientific feedback. Therefore we have summarised the key studies that have led to the validity and reliability development of the Team Management Index. The research statistics on the other instruments are available in the TMS Handbook from the distributors listed at the end of this book.

[120]

Means and intercorrelations of the Team Management Index (TMI) construct scales

Normative psychological instruments are usually based upon construct scales which measure independent characteristics about the respondents. Therefore to be reliable it is important that the scales chosen are more or less unrelated to each other. The test for independent scales is the Pearson product-moment coefficient, sometimes called the scale intercorrelation coefficient.

We report here some data on scale characteristics, based on a sample of 275 respondents who completed the personal Team Management Index. Mean ages of the sampling ranged from 19 to 64 with a standard deviation of 7.8. Eleven per cent of the sample were female, with 28 per cent filling out the TMI in Australia, 7 per cent in Asia, and 66 per cent in the UK. They worked in a variety of management positions ranging from accounting (25 per cent) to engineering (18 per cent) and computing (11 per cent).

Table 1 presents data relating to the intercorrelations and to the central tendency.

The means of the various scales reveal the differing central tendencies. E-I and P-C have distributions which cluster roughly around the mid-point of zero. The S-F scale mean suggests that a few more people are scoring on the structured side of the scale (1 to +30) than the flexible side (-30 to -1). The A-B scale mean suggests a more definite preference of the sample for analytical rather than beliefs-based decision-making. This same tendency has occurred on larger samples and our most recent data base of 7000 managers shows means of 4.1 for the S-F scale and 11.8 for the A-B scale. This is not surprising given that much of our data is collected from people in international business organisations which in general show a preference for analytical and structured 'cultures'. Managers in these organisations are often trained to be analytical and structured as that is the way these businesses tend to operate.

The continuous Pearson product-moment coefficients are also shown in Table 1. The results confirm the relative independence of the scales. E-1 is moderately negatively related to P-C (-0.34) while P-C is moderately positively related to A-B and S-F (0.32 and 0.32). A-B is moderately positively related to S-F (0.32) while E-1 and S-F are fairly independent (-0.13). However, the two most closely related scales E-I and P-C share only 12 per cent common variance, and the scales can be considered to be relatively independent.

	Mean*	PC	AB	SF
Extroversion-introversion	.43	-34	-22	-13
Practical-creative	1.17		32	32
Analytical-beliefs-based	11.34			32
Structured-flexible	4.86			

*Note: Scales range from -30 for the second mentioned pole (i.e. I, C, B and F) to +30 for the first mentioned pole (E, P, A and S).

Table 1. Means and intercorrelations of scales.

Relationship of the four constructs to the Types of Work model

The four constructs (E-I, P-C, A-B and S-F) can be considered to be 'at right angles in four-dimensional space'. However, we were able to take a two-dimensional slice through this space and map it closely to the Types of Work model. This technique is called factor analysis and is quite complicated mathematically. Here we will show the end results of the technique but further information and confirmation of our results is presented in the work by Davies (1988).

[122]

The four constructs project on to the Types of Work model approximately as shown in Figure 17. The E-I axis separates the Promoting-Developing and Maintaining-Inspecting sectors. The A-B axis separates the Developing-Organising and Advising-Maintaining sectors, the P-C axis separates the Inspecting-Producing and Innovating-Exploring and the S-F axis separates the Producing-Organising and Innovating-Advising sectors.

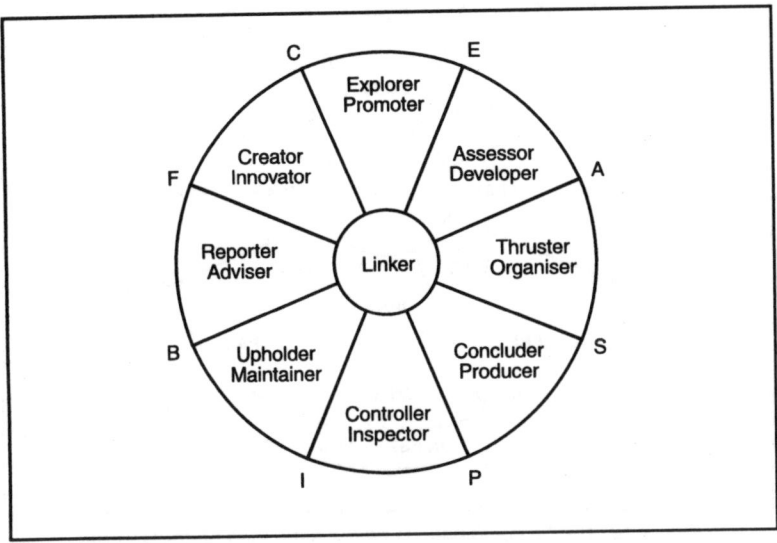

Figure 17. The constructs mapped on to the types of work model.

As a result of this arrangement the 16 dichotomous combinations of the scales map into each sector as shown in Figure 18.

As can be seen, two work preference combinations define each Team Role on the Wheel. Thus Explorer-Promoters are extrovert and creative, Assessor-Developers are extrovert and analytical, Thruster-Organisers are analytical and structured, Concluder-Producers are practical and structured, Controller-Inspectors are introverted and practical, Upholder-Maintainers are introverted and beliefs-based, Reporter-Advisers are beliefs-based and flexible, and Creator-Innovators are creative and flexible. These common shared work preferences give each sector its predominant characteristics.

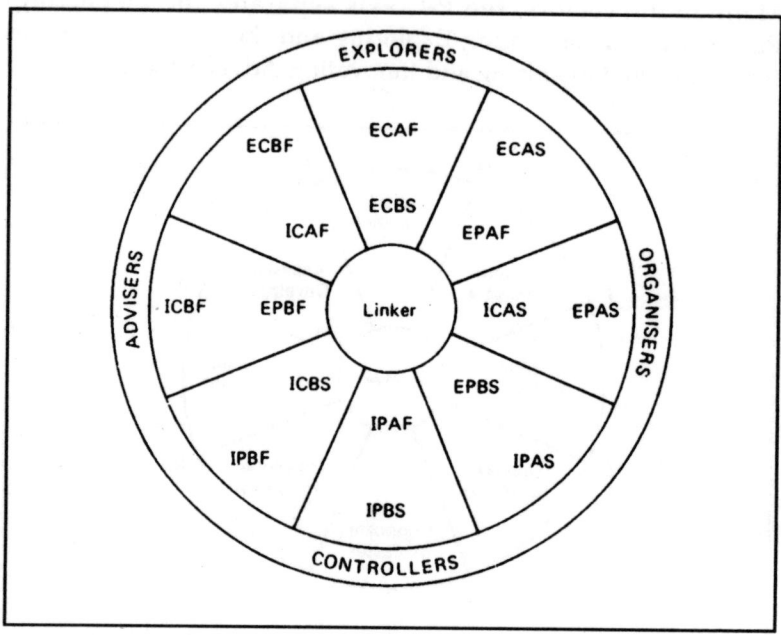

Figure 18. The 16 combinations on the team management wheel.

As well as the similarities there are key differences reflecting the different ways that Reporter-Advisers or Thruster-Organisers, for example, go about their work. The introverted and creative Reporter-Advisers are more likely to gather information from consulting the literature or reading manuals and looking for the conceptual approach, whereas the extroverted and practical Reporter-Advisers are more likely to gather information from a network of acquaintances or from travelling around and meeting people. The extroverted and practical Thruster-Organisers will be more present-oriented and want to see results today whereas the introverted and creative Thruster-Organisers will enjoy thinking about tomorrow but keep their thoughts to themselves. When the introverted and creative Thruster-Organisers have moved to a stage where they really believe in their thoughts then they will jump into action and want things done 'yesterday'.

Distribution of team roles

It is interesting to examine the distribution of team roles that we have found in working with managers all over the world. Looking at a data base of 7000 managers, the distributions are shown in Figure 19. The various sectors relate to the combinations shown in Figure 18.

Their first role preference maps 63 per cent of the managers into the AS sectors of the Wheel. As mentioned previously, we believe that this reflects the culture present in many of the international organisations of today, and the requirements expected of middle managers. Noticeable differences do occur, however, in several of the hi-tech organisations. In Hewlett-Packard laboratories, for example, 23 per cent of a sample of 132 managers tested mapped into the Creator-innovator sector as compared with an average of 9 per cent for the pooled data shown in Figure 12.

It is interesting to reflect on the low numbers of managers mapping into the Reporter-Adviser and Upholder-Maintainer sectors. Typically, many managers with these preferences seek 'staff' positions rather than 'line' positions and as there are many more line managers than staff 'advisers' it is not surprising to obtain this result.

[125]

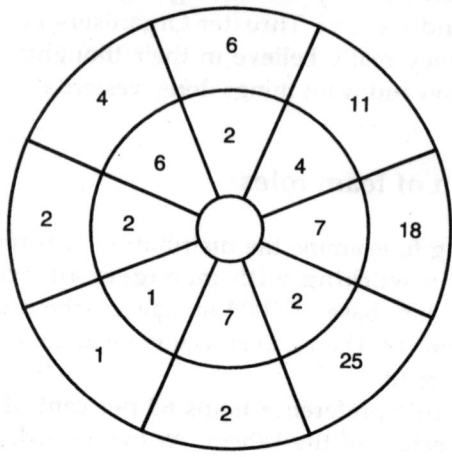

Figure 19.

How reliable is the Team Management Index?

Reliability addresses the problem of random error in measurement. A reliable instrument should therefore give similar scores if a respondent completed it at different times, despite differences in his/her motivation, the weather, etc. The items that make up the scale should also be consistent in the constructs they are measuring.

If an individual completing the TMI scored E-20 one day and E-2 two weeks later, we might begin to question how accurate the TMI is in measuring extroversion-introversion. Knowing that a score can vary from I-30 to E-30 (consisting of 61 points) then such a variation can seem quite large. Of course, such a difference is not as large as if a respondent had scored E-20 on one occasion and I-20 on the next. One day we would be saying that he or she is an extrovert and the next an introvert. Considering that the instrument is meant to measure consistent and relatively

enduring predispositions, we would rightly question its reliability.

There are a variety of ways in which reliability can be reported.
Most common is the reliability coefficient. Coefficients range from
0 to 1.0 with a reliability of 1.0 indicating lack of measurement
error (a perfectly reliable measure), and 0 indicating a completely
unreliable measure (all variance is due to error).

Two estimates of reliability (split-half and alpha coefficients)
computed on the sample of 275 managers described above are
shown in Table 2 for each of the four continuous sub-scales of the
TMI. Also supplied are KR-20 coefficients which analyse the reliability of the scales as dichotomous scales. KR-20 estimates are
usually smaller as they take into account less information, but are
more appropriate when we view the scales as dichotomous rather
than continuous. These estimates are usually referred to as
'internal consistency' measures as they index the consistency of
items that make up a scale. Coefficients of this magnitude are
usually viewed as adequate for a test from the affective domain,
especially given the short length of the sub-scales.

Sub-scale	Alpha	Split-half	KR-20
E-I	.83	.81	.81
P-C	.85	.88	.83
A-B	.86	.86	.85
S-F	.80	.84	.77

Table 2. Reliability of TMI sub-scales.

Split-half reliability, KR-20 and alpha coefficients measure random
error due to internal sources only. While these are accepted as the
major source of random error variance, error due to external
sources also needs to be investigated.

Test-retest reliability assesses the temporal stability of a
measure. It can tap sources of error external to the actual test such
as emotions, health, recording errors, etc. The length of time

between testings varies from study to study but short periods will be subject to bias from 'remembering' effects and longer periods will be subject to the fact that people do change, as we have stressed in previous chapters. Therefore a change in scores may reflect legitimate changes in the true score rather than random error. However, as it has been stated earlier that the TMI measures fairly permanent phenomena, we would expect the 'coefficient of stability' to be fairly high.

A sample of 44 managers completed the TMI on two occasions, at intervals varying from 6 to 7 months. Their scores on the second administration were correlated with their scores the first time they filled out the TMI. The resultant test-retest coefficients were 0.85 (Extroversion-Introversion), 0.76 (Practical-Creative), 0.70 (Analytical-Beliefs) and 0.67 (Structured-Flexible), giving a median reliability of 0.73. Retest coefficients of the continuous scales therefore demonstrate that the TMI has adequate stability over a 6-month period for this group.

Table 3 shows how profiles and categories changed over the 6-7 months period. As can be seen, 55 per cent of respondents returned the same role preference. Also 95 per cent of respondents swapped preferences once or less, demonstrating the considerable stability of the TMI roles over 6-7 months.

The results show that managers can be fairly sure of the stability of role profiles over short periods. Role preferences do not seem subject to wild fluctuations within such time spans. Where role preferences did change, only once did the person's role preference move to a non-adjacent sector on the Team Management Wheel and this was caused by two work preferences changing to their opposite poles. These people had low numeric scores on both administrations.

	Number	per cent
No change in overall profile	24	55
No change in EI preference	38	86
No change in PC preference	36	82
No change in AB preference	43	98
No change in SF preference	36	82
One preference change	18	41
Two preference changes	2	5
Three preference changes	0	0
Four preference changes	0	0

Table 3. Stability of team role preferences over six-seven months.

In summary then, reliability tells how confident we are that an individual profile or observed score reflects the true profile/score. We estimate this correspondence by methods which estimate random measurement error due to a variety of factors which affect the instrument's consistency and reliability. Reliability is an essential quality of any test from which important decisions and inferences are to be drawn.

How valid is the TMI?

While reliability is concerned with the ability of the TMI to measure role preferences with minimal random error, validity concentrates on the extent to which role preferences, as measured by the TMI, are meaningful.

When we move from assessing reliability to the validity of an indicator, we may use what are called 'external criteria'. External criteria are other indicators or more direct measures that have been found from past experiences and research to be strongly related (negatively as well as positively) to the concept we are trying to measure.

To the extent that the indicator shows a strong and consistent relationship to appropriate external criteria, we say that it has some degree of validity.

[129]

Team Management

Assessing the validity of an indicator is a long-term process involving the 'testing out' of hypotheses regarding structure and utility. As such, validity studies are an ongoing part of our work and we welcome enquiries from any researchers who wish to become involved. Some results of our validity studies are presented in Davies (1988).

Most respondents to date have provided information relating to the activities they engage in as part of their management and professional roles. Where a substantial number have been able to be placed into discrete categories, occupational profiles have been developed. While there is not enough space to show all the data here, we have picked two profiles at random – one for those managers working in Production, Construction and Control (Figure 20) and one for those working in Personnel and Training (Figure 21).

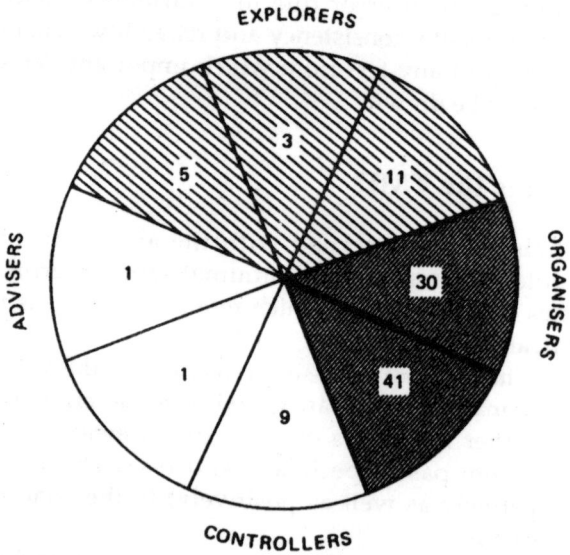

Figure 20. Role preference of managers working in production, construction and control (n = 465).

Each occupational profile consists of a description of the functional or professional area of the group of managers included in the profile. This is followed by the number included in the sample. Underneath this is a simplified diagram of the Team Management Wheel. For the sake of clarity the names of the eight role preferences are omitted; however, the roles are in the usual positions (i.e. Explorer-Promoter at the north, Controller-Inspector at the south, Reporter-Advisers and Thruster-Organisers on the left and right respectively).

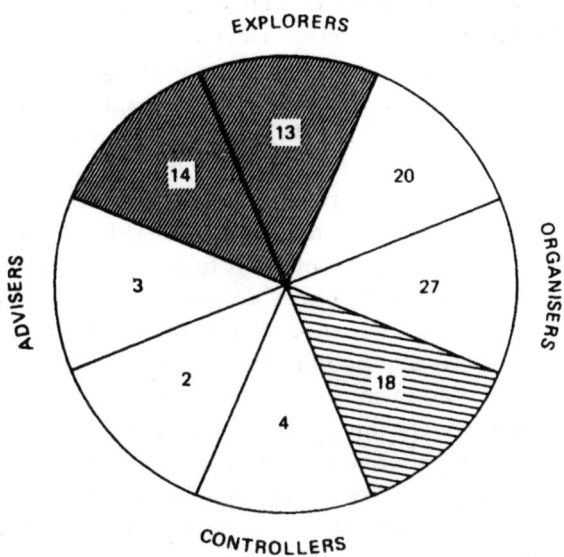

Figure 21. Role preference of managers working in personnel and training (n = 496).

The figure in each of the segments relates to the proportion of the relevant sample that returned the appropriate profile. For example, among managers working in production, construction or control areas, 41 per cent were Concluder-Producers while only 3 per cent were Explorer-Promoters.

[131]

Team Management

A chi-square procedure was utilised to test for significant differences between the relevant proportion and what we would expect from the whole sample ($p < 0.05$). Where there is significantly more than we would expect, the role preference is heavily shaded. Where there is less, the role preference is lightly shaded. Where there is not a large enough difference to be statistically significant, there is no shading.

The two functional areas illustrated show a marked difference in their role preference make-up. Concluder-Producers are well represented among managers working in Production, Construction and Control while there are less Creator-Innovators, Explorer-Promoters and Assessor-Developers. Among Personnel and Training Managers almost the opposite situation exists. There are less Concluder-Producers but a heavier weighting towards the Explorer-Adviser part of the Wheel. Creator-Innovators and Explorer-Promoters are more numerous than we would expect, given the distribution of role preferences among the total sample.

These profiles indicate that managers with different role preferences seem to be attracted to different functional areas and types of work tasks. Work preferences *do* seem to be related to the current functional areas of managers. Further research is proposed to test the hypothesis that people with certain role preferences are more likely to succeed in some areas than others.

Davies (1988) shows the functional areas most highly represented for each role preference. There is a noticeable 'clustering' of similar managerial activities in certain sectors of the Wheel. To a large extent, these are consistent with the defining characteristics of the corresponding role preference. To illustrate this, let us examine each team role in turn, from the north (Exploring) sectors, around to the south (Controlling) sectors and back to the north.

- *Explorer-Promoters*
  Corporate planning and development managers and those involved in design or research and development often have this as a major role preference.

[132]

- *Assessor-Developers*
  A popular profile among sales and marketing managers. Also chairmen, directors and proprietors (27 per cent) often have this role preference.

- *Thruster-Organisers*
  Sales and marketing people often map into this area, as do production, construction and control managers.

- *Concluder-Producers*
  Many finance and accounting managers (33 per cent) occupy this space as do, of course, production, construction and control managers (41 per cent).

- *Controller-Inspectors*
  No single functional area dominates, but it includes many finance and accounting managers (10 per cent), production, construction and control managers (9 per cent) and administration managers (8 per cent).

- *Upholder-Maintainers*
  Managers working in administrative positions are the only significant group with this role preference.

- *Reporter-Advisers*
  Many of the Reporter-Advisers tested were working in management consultant roles as well as personnel and training, and corporate planning and development.

- *Creator-Innovators*
  Predictably, managers working in design or research and development predominate in this role. Management consultants are also significant in this role.

Comparison with MBTI

Of interest to many is the relationship of the TMI constructs to the Myers-Briggs Type Indicator (Form G) constructs. These have been examined for convergent discriminant validity on a sample of 88 managers, using the Campbell-Fiske multi-trait, multi-method matrix (Table 4).

E-I								
P-C	-41							
A-B	-20	-30						
S-F	-18	46	27					
E-I	62	-05	10	04				
S-N	-30	67	21	28	03			
T-F	-11	20	56	14	08	38		
J-P	-36	42	12	27	13	51	31	
	E-I	**P-C**	**A-B**	**S-F**	**E-I**	**S-N**	**T-F**	**J-P**

Table 4. Campbell-Fiske multi-method matrix (n = 88, 20% female).

In this Table the lower half of the correlation matrix is reproduced. As can be seen, there is a substantial relationship between three convergent validity coefficients (E-I/E-I, P-C/S-N, A-B/T-F) while there is a slight relationship between J-P and S-F. These coefficients indicate that there is only 39 per cent shared variance between E-I/E-I; 45 per cent between P-C/S-N; 31 per cent between A-B/T-F and 7 per cent between J-P and S-F.

Several heterotrait-heteromethod correlations approach or exceed these coefficients as do heterotrait-monomethod coefficients.

In summary then, it would be hard to mount an argument that the scales of each instrument are measuring the same construct since the shared variances together with the random internal error of the instrument account for only 30-75 per cent of the difference, depending on which construct is considered. There is enough evidence to show that, especially in the case of the J-P/S-F relationship, the Team Management Index and the MBTI (Form G) are

[134]

measuring constructs that hold some elements in common but which are substantially different.

The reasons for this difference, we believe, can be explained by the different approaches people have to the *work* and *non-work* situation. Several people in our comparison study were *extroverted* and *structured* at work but *introverted* and *perceiving* on the MBTI. When questioned, they indicated that they had learned over the years to adopt a more outgoing relationship with customers and colleagues and to work in a structured way. These characteristics were a part of the company culture in the organisations concerned and the people had learned to behave in a way that led to 'rewards'. This had therefore become their preferred way of working. Other people were *introverted* and *sensing* on the MBTI and yet showed a preference for *Exploring* work (*extroverted* and *creative* on the TMI). In these and similar cases *work* and *non-work* were two distinct compartments of their lives and they sought a balance between the two.

The whole subject of work and non-work is a fascinating area of research. For those who are interested we refer you to the review article by Kabanoff (1980).

Our work therefore supports the view that people conform with certain role requirements at work which are different from those they exhibit at home. Moreover, we would suggest that where the role preferences and the role required are substantially different, then *stress* leading to some form of tension will occur. This may manifest itself in withdrawal symptoms, job dissatisfaction, medical problems or other symptoms of tension.

Therefore a further stage in the development of our work on Team Management is to look at the issues arising in a mismatch between people's work preferences and their work role. How do people adjust? How do teams resolve the problem of the 'round peg in the square hole'? A clearer understanding of these issues will be of considerable benefit not only to the individuals, but to the total management of individual and team performance. This can be done by gaining feedback on the Types of Work Index and comparing your results with your TMI scores.

HIGH-PERFORMING TEAMS

Why teams fail and succeed

We have already indicated in earlier chapters some of the reasons why teams fail. Many of these teams are unbalanced, with team members having the same 'view of the world' – that is, they all map into the same part of the Team Management Wheel. As a result they often miss opportunities and suffer from 'group-think'.

Many teams fail because no one is doing the linking. Even the most perfectly balanced team can be a dismal failure if effort is not put into applying the skills of linking, which is often more difficult than when the team is unbalanced.

In addition we have noticed other behaviours of teams which give us a further insight into some of the reasons as to why they fail to perform at a high level.

Improving relationship management

If everyone wants to talk and no one is prepared to listen then often the team will fail. When people behave in an extremely extroverted way at meetings, it can be difficult to get things done in an orderly way. Many people will be interrupting, very often speaking in order to think.

Therefore at meetings it is important to get the balance right between the *extroverts* and the *introverts*. If you allow the extroverts to dominate you will be acting on information from only one part of the team and the valuable contributions which often come from more introverted people will not be forthcoming. The introverts will very likely 'switch off' and wonder why they ever come to these meetings. The chairperson of team meetings needs to act very much as a linker, making sure that the extroverts are controlled and the introverts persuaded to contribute. If a balanced contribution can be extracted from all members, then everyone will feel valued and better decisions will result.

Sometimes the effectiveness of meetings can be improved by asking people to prepare papers for discussion prior to a meeting. Introverts will usually welcome this as it gives them a chance to get their thoughts in order. Extroverts, however, may have to be persuaded of the benefits of this approach as they may prefer to speak 'off-the-cuff'. While they can be very effective interacting in this way they may get off the subject and therefore need to be encouraged to stick to the point.

Introverts like to think before they speak. If you ask too many open-ended questions such as 'What does everyone think about that?', it will usually be the extroverts who will respond because they will want to talk out loud to get their thoughts in order. To get the contributions from introverts you may need to call on them by name. One approach that often works is to say, 'Well, we've all heard what Judith and Jim have to say; what do you think about it, David?' The meeting is then cleared for David (more introverted) to make his contribution.

Another way of bringing life to a quiet meeting is to clearly identify the question to be considered, and ask for each person's views in turn. Once you have got the views you can identify what facts there are to support the opinions. Then get back to people and ask them what they think should be done as a function of the opinions they have.

Improving information management

Sometimes people will concentrate too heavily on details. They will want to know too many facts and therefore get bogged down in specifics. While this can be useful it may well indeed miss the general point of trying to reach an understanding of the overall picture. Meetings like this become too *practical*.

In your role as a linker you therefore need to get people to consider the implication of the detail. Ask people what must be done and who must do it if you are to achieve the objectives. Don't get buried in a mass of data. Ask people what the implications of the facts are and then get them to take accountability for results.

On other occasions you have the opposite problem to the practical meeting in that people will be full of ideas. Meetings like this can often be too *creative*. These meetings are usually very exciting and full of energy but often weak on the outputs. If this is the case, it may be necessary to get people to think through their ideas and ask them how they will work in practice. Usually, though, they will be short of data. Therefore ensure that between the first and second meeting people actually go out and get the facts. Don't let them get away with 'woolly thinking'. Tie them down by questions such as, 'How would it work in practice?' or 'What do you believe you could do to improve the situation?'

Creative meetings are very valuable but they must produce a result. It is your job as a linker to ensure that outputs occur.

Improving decision-making

Here there may be an overemphasis on logic and objectivity. People will behave in a very rational way and will try to reach decisions on the basis of facts. This can be extremely valuable providing it doesn't overlook the key values and principles. Your job as a linker is to get people to consider not only the facts of the situation but the principles involved. Ask people questions, such as 'Is that approach fair?' or 'Is that approach going to achieve our wider objectives?'

Team values are an important contributor to high performance. If team members share the same underlying values and principles, often they will work harder to achieve the goals. If you have not already done so then get your team together for a special meeting to discuss the values that are important to each individual.

In contrast, some teams may overemphasise their beliefs and convictions when discussing decisions to be made. These meetings will often have an 'evangelical' flavour about them. Other people may be swept up in a general feeling of righteousness and everyone feels good about the decision.

This may happen in meetings on such matters as safety, or improving working conditions, or giving to charity. These things can be very worthwhile, but before a decision is made the 'analytical' side of the equation needs to be examined. Questions such as 'What will be the cost of this effort?' or 'How can we make this work in practice?' or 'What will we get out of this?' need to be posed.

Improving organisation

Here the weakness can be people seeking to reach decisions before they have enough information. There will be strong views put forward by people who feel they know what is best for the situation. Things will be too *structured*.

If you are chairing a situation like this you need to open up the meeting and diverge the discussion rather than allowing it to converge too quickly. Questions such as, 'What other information

[139]

do we need before coming to a decision?' or 'How will this affect our other operation?' can be very useful.

In contrast you can have a meeting that is too flexible, where people may be putting off a decision. People will talk around the issue rather than coming to a firm decision. Here your job as a linker is to get people to realise the importance of reaching a conclusion. You need to converge the meeting rather than allow it to diverge.

This can be done by setting deadlines, perhaps by saying, 'The decision must be made before the end of the meeting', or indicating to people the criteria upon which the decision should be made, when the results are required by, and the time they have available to work on them.

The principles of high-performing teams (HPT principles)

In our research we spoke to many successful teams in both the private and public sectors. As a result of what managers told us we were able to group the data into eleven principles which seem to recur time and time again in high-performing teams. As part of a team-planning exercise it can be valuable to get team members to assess how your team fares on each principle. The principles and brief comments are listed below:

1　HPTs have a linker as a key team member

This has emerged in most teams as a critical factor. You need to assess your own group and ask: Who does the linking work? How is it done? How could it be improved? In most cases it should be the leader, but many teams work well where linking is shared.

2 HPTs set high output targets and regularly achieve them

Expectations are important. Effective team managers get the team to raise its game. They indicate that high quality and quantity can be achieved and reinforce success by positive feedback.

3 HPTs gain a high degree of job satisfaction from their work

Note that high job satisfaction comes from challenging work where high expectations have been met. Satisfaction follows successful work. It is little use getting people satisfied first. Challenging work must come first.

4 Team members of HPTs cooperate well with one another

We have found that the level of cooperation and *esprit de corps* is strong amongst HPTs. People work to help each other. Where this does not happen the manager wants to know why and acts to improve cooperation.

5 The managers of HPTs are well respected by the members for the example they set

Managers of HPTs are seen to do what they say. In particular they fulfil promises and lead by example.

6 HPTs are well balanced with respect to the roles people play in relation to their skills

Although teams did not always know their team management profiles, we found that those working well had naturally found a 'balance'. The feedback of Team Management Profiles reinforced what they were doing.

7   HPTs have a high degree of autonomy

Teams that were successful seemed to have more discretion in the way they were allowed to organise themselves.

8   HPTs learn quickly from their mistakes

There was a concentrated effort on learning and putting things right. One team had a series of meetings based on 'what we have learned' project papers, based on real cases.

9   HPTs are client-orientated

The teams we studied made every effort to identify whom they were serving, whether internally or externally, and met their needs. In the terms of Peters and Waterman (1982) they kept close to the customer and fulfilled their needs.

10   HPTs have high problem-solving skills and regularly review their performance

It was noticeable that the HPTs had effective meetings. The paperwork was well prepared in advance, the discussion concentrated on the issues, people tried to resolve issues rather than score points.

11   HPTs are motivated

Overall we were impressed with the keenness and enthusiasm shown in HPTs. They were keen to succeed. They worked hard. They saw their work as an exciting challenge.

The use of the principles in teamwork

We have used these principles as a way of getting the team to rate its performance, on a scale of 1 to 7, for each of the HPT

[142]

principles. Principles that the team rates low can then be used as a starting point for discussion.

This is a useful way to help identify the issues that need to be considered and helps the manager to develop a more effective team. However, this process is not a solution in itself. It is vital that the manager and the team are prepared to do something about the areas that score low and reinforce those that score high.

The manager must therefore work with the team to agree on how to improve each of the areas. This can be done by asking each member of the group to write down any ideas they may have for tackling a difficult area.

If, for example, the linking function is not being done satisfactorily then people should indicate what they would like to see. Each of the ideas should be listed and discussed by all. Once a suggested solution has been agreed a person's name should be put alongside it to implement action. At the subsequent meetings that person should be charged with reporting progress. In this way a team can improve its performance quite dramatically in a short period of time.

In conclusion

In this book we have brought together the key aspects of our research over the past eight years. The principles are simple, but if applied can lead to a quantum change in team performance. The major points we have made are:

- People are different and approach work in different ways. Successful managers understand these differences and make use of them in the way they manage.
- Differences manifest themselves in *work preferences* which can be measured by an adaptation of the four Jungian constructs to the workplace. The measures we use are extroversion-intro-

version, practical-creative, analytical-beliefs, and structured-flexible. People's score on each of these is measured by the Team Management Index.

- Work preferences can be mapped on to the Team Management Wheel, a cognitive aid to help managers look at the balance in their team.
- High-performing teams usually have a reasonable balance of team role preferences. This leads to multiple descriptions in problem-solving and will prevent group-think from occurring.
- In a balanced team, however, conflict will be incipient as people will be continually putting forward opposing view-points. This is essential to the generation of the 'best' decision but unless the process is well managed even balanced teams can fail.
- Therefore the two conditions which have to be fulfilled as a prerequisite for high-performance are (1) team balance and (2) first-class linking. However, when the balance is there it is often doubly hard to link the team together because of the different work preferences of the members. Teams which can achieve *both conditions* often generate outstanding results.
- The 'teamwork technology' contained in the Team Management Index, the Team Management Profiles and the Team Management Wheel can be used to design management systems to improve all aspects of the management role – from recruitment and selection through to team problem-solving.
- Critical success factors in a job can be measured by the Types of Work Index.
- Team performance can be evaluated in terms of nine key factors, measured by the Team Performance Index.
- Linking skills can be assessed by rating individuals against eleven key skills, using the Linking Skills Index.

We wish you well in your journey as a manager and hope to see you some day on one of our Team Management Workshops.

REFERENCES

Bales, R. *Interaction Process Analysis*, Addison Wesley, 1950.

Barnard, C. *The Functions of the Executive*, Harvard University Press, 1938.

Belbin, M. *Management Teams*, Butterworth-Heinemann, 1981.

Campbell, D. T., and Fiske, D. W. 'Convergent and Discriminant Validation by the Multitrait-Multimethod Matrix', *Psychological Bulletin*, vol. 56, pp. 81-105, 1959.

Cartwright, D., and Zander, A. 'Power and Influence in Groups' in *Groups in Group Dynamics Research and Theory*, Harper & Row, 1968.

Davies, R. V. *The Team Management Handbook*, TMS Development International, York, 1989 and 1993.

Deutsch, M. 'The Effects of Cooperation and Competition upon Group Processes', *Human Relations*, vol. 2, 1949.

Eysenck, H. *Psychology is about People*, Penguin Books, 1977.

Iacocca, L. *Iacocca – An Autobiography*, Bantam Books, 1986.

Team Management

Janis, I. L. *Victims of Group Think*, Houghton Mifflin, 1972.

Jung, C. J. *Psychological Types*, Routledge & Kegan Paul, 1923.

Kabanoff, B. 'Work and Nonwork – A Review of Models, Methods and Findings', *Psychological Bulletin*, vol. 88, pp. no. 1, 60-77, 1980.

Likert, R., and Likert, J. *New Ways of Managing Conflict*, McGraw-Hill, 1976.

McCann, D. J. *How to Influence Others at Work*, Butterworth-Heinemann, 1988.

McDonald, J. *The Game of Business*, Doubleday New York, 1975, ch. 9, 'Walt Disney'.

Margerison, C. J. *If Only I Had Said...*, Management Books 2000, 1987.

Margerison, C. J., and McCann, D. J. *How to Lead a Winning Team*, MCB University Press, 1985.

Margerison, C. J., and McCann, D. J. *The Team Management Index, The Types of Work Index, The Team Performance Index, The Linking Skills Index* – TMS Development International, York, 1993, and TMS (USA) Washington, 1993.

Margerison, C. J., and McCann, D. J. *How to Improve Team Management*, MCB University Press, 1989.

Myers-Briggs, J. *The Myers-Briggs Type Indicator*, Consulting Psychologists Press, 1976.

Shaw, M. Group Dynamics, *The Psychology of Small Group Behavior*, McGraw-Hill, 1981.

Smale, J. 'Behind the Brands of P & G', Interview between J. Smale and Priscilla Hayes-Petty, *Harvard Business Review*, vol. 63, no. 6, 1985.

REFERENCES

Weber, M. 'Types of Authority', in H. Gerth and C. Mills, *From Max Weber*, Oxford University Press, 1946.

Weber, M. *The Theory of Social and Economic Organization*, Glencoe Free Press, 1947.

Weick, K. E. *The Theory of Social and Economic Organization*, Addison Wesley, 1979.

Zander, A. *Making Groups Effective*, Jossey Bass, 1982.

THE TEAM MANAGEMENT INDEXES

Relevant, reliable feedback is essential in order to improve performance. Team Management Systems have produced well tested instruments in the following areas:

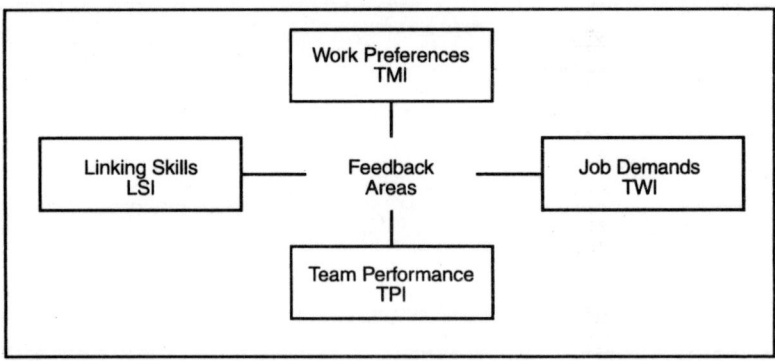

The Team Management Index (TMI) was created by Charles Margerison and Dick McCann to help managers develop their team management skills. It is now widely used in many countries throughout the world. If you would like to complete the index and receive a computerised report about your work preferences, leadership skills, and decision-making, please contact one of the organisations below.

Recent developments in the use of the Margerison-McCann Team Management Wheel have produced new exciting instruments which provide feedback that is helpful in the work situation.

The Linking Skills Index (LSI) provides a way in which other members of your team can assess your linking skills. The information you receive provides the basis for clarifying how others see you and improving relationships at work.

The Types of Work Index (TWI) is designed to help you identify the key demands of your job in the context of the Team Management Wheel. By comparing this measure with that from the Team Management Index Profile you can see the areas of similarity or difference between what you want and what the job provides. This measure is proving very helpful in recruitment and selection procedures and career counselling and planning.

The Team Performance Index (TPI) enables team members, their supervisors, their clients and colleagues to provide feedback on how they see the team's performance.

Overall the Team Management Wheel and the associated measures and profiles have proved easy-to-use techniques for improving people's understanding of how to work together more effectively.

United Kingdom and rest of Europe

Ms Cathy Hick
TMS Development International Ltd
128 Holgate Road
York
North Yorkshire
YO2 4DL
(Tel. 01904-641640)
(Fax. 01904-640076)

United States of America

Jan Bearce
TMS (USA) Inc
11718, Bowman Green Drive
Reston,
Virginia 22090
(Tel. 703 318-7206)
(Fax. 703 318-9527)

Australia and the rest of the world

Team Management Systems
PO Box 1107
Milton
Brisbane
Queensland 4064
Australia
(Tel. 07-368-2333)
(Fax. 07-368-2311)

INDEX

DBD/03/03/05